Peninsula
· Roots ·

A Delmarva Miscellany

Peninsula
· Roots ·
A Delmarva Miscellany

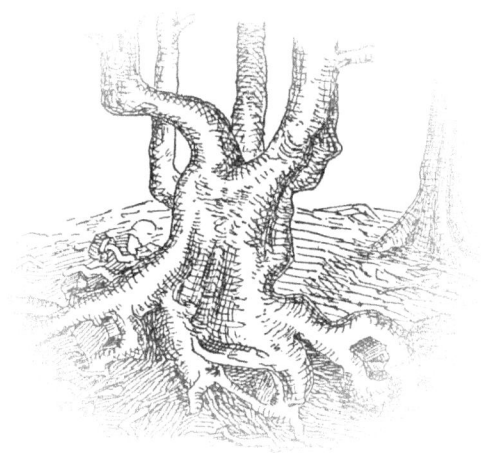

Christopher Slavens

Bald Cypress Books
Laurel, Delaware

baldcypressbooks.com

Copyright © 2022 Christopher Slavens.
All rights reserved.

ISBN: 978-1-7361370-5-5

Library of Congress Control Number: 2021925760

Publisher's Cataloging-in-Publication Data

Slavens, Christopher, author.
Peninsula Roots: A Delmarva Miscellany / Christopher Slavens.
First trade paperback original edition.
Laurel, DE: Bald Cypress Books, 2022.
LCCN: 2021925760 | ISBN: 978-1-7361370-5-5
Delmarva Peninsula—History.
Delmarva Peninsula—Genealogy.
Delaware—History. | Nanticoke Indians.

Cover image: Illustration of tree roots resisting lateral forces by
A. Errich, *Popular Science Monthly*, 1911. Public domain.

For Grandma

Contents

Introduction	i
A Brief History of Broad Creek Town	1
The Nanticokes' Last Stand	7
"Sockum" and the Nanticokes of Broad Creek	13
James Sockam of Dagsborough Hundred	17
The Sockum Family: Further Research	19
Regua, Rigware, Ridgeway: The Evolution of a Mysterious Surname	31
Broad Creek Bridge and the Old Forge	41
Jarrett Willey, Innholder at Broad Creek	47
Laurel's Forgotten House of Worship?	49
Blackfoot Town (Dagsboro) in Colonial Primary Sources	53

Parramore's Plantation at Whaley's Crossroads	57
Reclaiming Delaware's Unsavory Place-Names: The Whorekill	63
Reclaiming Delaware's Unsavory Place-Names: Murderkill	67
Delaware Day: *Not* the First State	71
Reverend Richard F. Cadle	75
The Journal of Rev. John Milton Purner	77
Old Forge A.M.E. Church & Camp	81
Terrapin Hill & Bull's Mills	85
A Brief History of Trap Pond	89
Red Hannah: Delaware's Whipping Post	93

Introduction

In March of 2014, I created a blog dedicated to Delmarva history, folklore, and genealogy, and temporarily titled it *Peninsula Roots*, always intending to rename it when I thought of something better. Whether because I couldn't think of anything better, or I didn't really try, the title stuck.

During the next several years, I wrote a variety of articles about local history, many of them based on original research. A series of articles about the Nanticoke Indians became rather popular, and I still receive emails from modern-day Nanticoke descendants, particularly those related to the fascinating Sockum family, thanking me for my research or seeking additional information. The WordPress interface I use to manage the site keeps track of the search terms which lead visitors to the site, and, to this day, the vast majority of them are related to Nanticoke history.

In 2016, I joined the Laurel Historical Society and began contributing to the organization's triannual newsletter. A couple of years later, I was invited to edit the newsletter. During the same period, I was researching and writing *The Roofed Graves of Delmarva*, which I published in 2020. *Peninsula Roots* fell by the wayside, for the most part, as I focused on other projects.

When I created a website and blog for Bald Cypress Books in 2020, I realized that my online presence was beginning to feel a bit scattered: Go to Facebook for this, LinkedIn for that, the historical society for my latest research article, the new website for publishing updates, the old website for increasingly rare articles that didn't fit into one of the other projects—it was too much for *me* to keep track of, let alone anybody else. I decided to discontinue *Peninsula Roots*, and herd all of the regular readers over to the Bald Cypress Books website.

However, I wanted to save the material I'd published previously, and realized that there was just enough of it to fill a book. A disorganized, fragmented book, perhaps, but a book nonetheless; a collection of this and that, odds and ends, articles and maps and photos. A miscellany.

During the process of editing the material from the blog, I updated some of the pieces as needed, and included additional material which had been published elsewhere, such as my articles for the historical society.

The articles in this book are not intended to offer the final word on any subject. In many cases, they are starting points; cautious forays into unexplored territory; preliminary investigations of poorly understood subjects which deserve far, far more research. In some cases, brief articles evolved into much more detailed works—some of which have not yet been published. For example, my early articles about Nanticoke Indian history and genealogy inspired a forthcoming book which answers many of the questions I wondered about several years ago, and I struggled to decide whether to include such outdated material in this book. In the end, I included most of it, while correcting outright errors.

It is my hope that some of the readers of this book will be inspired to dig deeper and write their own works about the fascinating roots of our cherished peninsula.

CHRISTOPHER SLAVENS
Laurel, Delaware
December 27, 2021

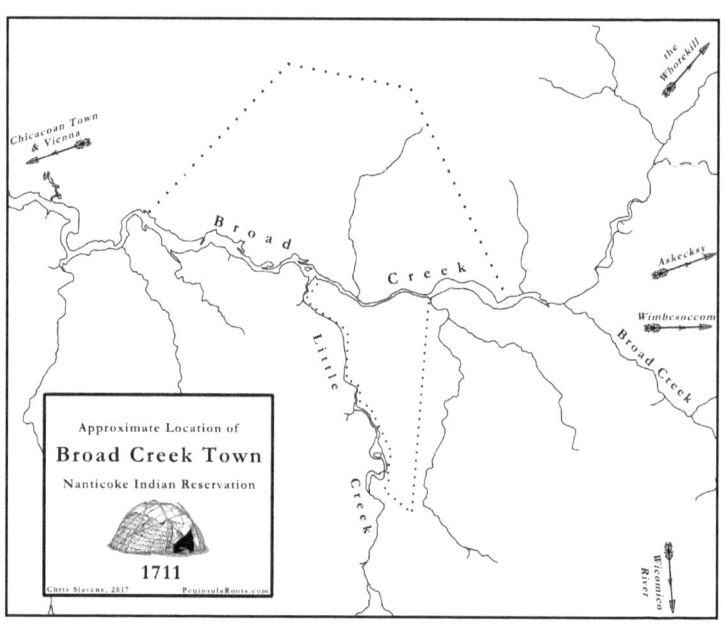

A Brief History of Broad Creek Town

May 2017

The Nanticoke Indians who moved to Broad Creek in or around 1705 were, in many ways, a defeated people. In the nearly one hundred years since their ancestors had welcomed Captain John Smith's barge with a barrage of arrows, their numbers, power, and wealth had diminished due to a series of wars and treaties. Even their reservation at the junction of the Nanticoke River and Chicacoan Creek was threatened by aggressive, trespassing English newcomers. This story would require many pages to tell. For the sake of brevity, suffice it to say that they were desperate and discouraged—but perhaps hopeful that they would be able to preserve their culture in their new home, farther inland with only a handful of English neighbors.

The refugees settled near a site known as the Wading Place, which was one of the easier points at which to cross Broad Creek. It is possible that there was already a village or camp there, although the records seem to imply that the location was a new one for the tribe. Whether there was an existing Nanticoke settlement at the site or not, the land on both sides of the creek had been granted to Englishmen in the 1680s. The Nanticokes might not have been aware of this—or they might not have cared. Evidently the English did care, and told the Nanticokes that they might have to relocate yet again, for in October of 1711, the Maryland legislature was informed that "the Nanticoke Indians are much dissatisfied they may not be permitted to continue at Broad Creek where they are set down…" Perhaps indicating that the dwindling tribe was still a force to be reckoned with, the provincial government decided it would be unwise to evict them, and instead empowered commissioners to purchase and reserve three thousand acres on Broad Creek for their use.

In a matter of weeks, surveyor William Whittington, Jr., laid out two tracts, one on each side of the creek. The northern tract consisted of the entire 2,500-acre tract known as Greenland, originally granted to William Green. The southern tract consisted of 500 acres on the east side of Little Creek, and included 133 acres of a tract known as Batchelor's Delight, originally surveyed for Col. William Stevens, but subsequently transferred to James Wythe and Marmaduke Master.

A jury of twelve local freeholders determined that Greenland was worth 50,000 pounds of tobacco; the portion of Batchelor's Delight, 2,666 pounds of tobacco; and the remainder of the southern tract, 7,334 pounds of tobacco. Additionally, they awarded Henry Freaks 3,000 pounds of tobacco "for his Damages in building Clearing and fencing on the said Land…" and William Denton, Jr., 500 pounds of tobacco "for his damages for work and repareing to build and setle on the Land…"

Since the English had a habit of unimaginatively (and often

misleadingly) naming any band of Indians after the waterway on which they lived, the Nanticokes on Broad Creek became known as the Broad Creek Indians, and their settlement was called Broad Creek Town. If they gave it a name of their own, it was never recorded.

Little is known of Broad Creek Town, other than its location. Was there a central village, or were the residents spread out? Did they live in traditional wigwams, or European-style cabins? We can't be sure, but the best guess is probably "all of the above." The historian J. Thomas Scharf later reported that they "cultivated the land to some extent" and built a "harbor." Additionally, they probably interacted with the residents of Askecksy, a nearby Indian River Indian reservation established at about the same time.

A little more is known of the leadership of the Broad Creek Indians, but not much. The records of the time mention a number of Nanticoke leaders—notably Panquash, whose leadership stretched from the 1690s into the 1740s—but rarely specify whether they were from Chicacoan or Broad Creek. One such leader was Rassekettham, who accompanied Panquash and Tom Coursey in 1713 to inform the English that the tribe no longer recognized its former emperor, Asquash, who had moved to Pennsylvania. They also inquired as to whether the English had conspired with Asquash to kill Panquash and Rassekettham, and were assured that they had not and would not. Though Rassekettham was not explicitly identified as a Broad Creek Indian, the tributary known as Rossakatum Creek or Rossakatum Branch is assumed to have been named after him. It is likely that he was the chief of the Broad Creek band in 1713.

Another probable leader was King Toby, who, with fellow Broad Creek Indians Lolloway and Whist, traveled to the county court held at Dividing Creek in 1725 to complain that some of the Caldwells had mistreated them in some way. Lolloway might have been the same Indian named Lolloway who had been assaulted so badly in Somerset Parish the previous year that he nearly died. Other incidents reported in and around the various Indian reservations indicate that tensions continued to escalate during this time.

In the spring of 1742, the Nanticokes, Choptanks, Indian River Indians, Pocomokes, and some visiting Shawnees met in Wimbesoccom Neck to discuss a plot to massacre the local settlers and reclaim the Eastern Shore, supposedly with the help of the Iroquois Confederacy and the French. The tale of "the plot in the swamp" has been told elsewhere, but a few details are worth noting. Wimbesoccom Neck consisted of the land east of Wimbesoccom Creek (today's Gray's Branch) and north of the main branch of Broad Creek, which flows through today's Trap Pond. The neck stretched into the outskirts of what would later be called Gumborough Hundred, and was probably heavily wooded and sparsely settled—an ideal location for a secret powwow. Interestingly, some of the Broad Creek Indians spoke of a "logged house" stocked with weapons, located a few miles into the swamp. Their leaders at this time were known as Simon Alsechqueck and Captain John.

But the plot was discovered and foiled, and numerous Indians arrested, and the tribal leaders were forced to sign an extremely restrictive treaty. Henceforth, the Nanticokes could no longer elect an emperor, and every member of the tribe was forbidden to own a gun without obtaining a license from the governor. It was the last straw. Just two years later, Simon Alsechqueck requested and received permission for the tribe to migrate north and live among the Iroquois, and by the 1750s, Broad Creek Town was said to be deserted.

In 1768, the provincial government authorized commissioners to sell what had become known as the Indian Lands, and according to later deeds, Joseph Forman purchased 518 acres at the western end of the northern tract, and John Mitchell purchased 2,236 acres. Barkley Townsend acquired part of the southern tract prior to 1776. Following Mitchell's death in 1787, his portion was sold to a number of buyers including George Mitchell, George Corbin, and John Creighton. Decades later, Forman's heirs divided his parcel into two lots and sold one to Dr. James Derickson, and the other to Benjamin Fooks and Kendall M. Lewis.

Today, the town of Laurel occupies much of the site of Broad Creek Town, and continues to grow, making archaeological investigation difficult. Even so, the stone artifacts that frequently turn up in nearby fields, and local names like Rossakatum and Sockum, survive to remind us of the first people to call Broad Creek home.

THE NANTICOKES' LAST STAND

Originally published by the *Laurel Star*
May 2015

WITH ABOUT 800 HOUSES on the National Register of Historic Places and more than a dozen historic churches in and around the town, Laurel is the kind of place where the past is not only remembered, but celebrated. Many local families can trace their roots back to the 18th century, and some still live on land cleared by their distant ancestors when the Delmarva Peninsula was a wild frontier. Yet one of the most significant and fascinating events in the area's history is also one of the least known, possibly because it took place when the area was claimed by Maryland.

Long before Barkley Townsend founded a town on the south side of Broad Creek and named it after the beautiful laurel bushes growing along the creek's banks, the Nanticokes thrived here. Their territory stretched from the Chesapeake Bay to the vast cypress swamp in the center of the peninsula, and was home to at least ten villages. Captain John Smith visited the tribe in June of 1608, and noted that they were rich in furs and shell money, and were "the best Marchants of all other Salvages."

In the following decades, the tribe listened to reports of European expansion, as the Dutch and Swedes settled in the northeast, and the English spread out from the western shore into Accomack and Choptank territory, and beyond. Attempts to resist ended badly. It was with this in mind, perhaps, that Unnacokasinnon, "Emperor of Nantecoke," signed a peace treaty in 1668. The treaty laid out several rules for the Nanticokes; among them, that they would be required to lay down their weapons if they crossed paths with Englishmen in the woods. Unnacokasinnon also promised to "deliver up" the neighboring Wicomisses, who were his subjects. A Wicomiss man had recently killed an English captain, possibly to avenge the death of his wife. The Wicomisses were subsequently destroyed.

In 1698, the Maryland legislature established a large reservation on Chicacoan Creek, but a few years later, at about the time that the town of Vienna was established nearby, most of the Nanticokes moved up the river to Broad Creek. Whether they reclaimed an old village, moved into an existing one, or established a new one is unclear. It seems that the move was prompted by a combination of English harassment and depleted resources. The legislature, reluctant to provoke the tribe, decided to create a second reservation rather than force them to leave. The Nanticoke village on Broad Creek became known as Broad Creek Town, and its residents were sometimes called the Broad Creek Indians. At that time, the area was part of Somerset County (Worcester and Wicomico Counties did not yet exist), and would not be ceded to Sussex County for nearly seventy years.

During the next three decades, many English settlers were granted land in the surrounding area. Most of them were tobacco planters from Maryland and Virginia, drawn to northern Somerset by affordable land. At that time, the territory east of Broad Creek Town was part of the immense Pocomoke Swamp. In addition to clearing the land of trees, the settlers had to drain it, which was accomplished with a network of ditches.

As more and more land was cleared and cultivated, the Nanticokes began to feel cornered. For generations they had lived in long-term villages along the coast, rivers, and creeks for most of the year, and periodically moved inland to hunt. Now they were more or less confined to their two reservations. Dishonest traders' use of alcohol to intoxicate them and trick them into unfair business transactions also fueled rising tensions between the peninsula Indians and their English neighbors. In 1721, some of the tribes even asked the English authorities to prevent traders from selling or giving them rum.

By the spring of 1742, the situation was nearing its breaking point, and when a party of twenty-some Shawnee visited Chicacoan Town to share news of a French and Iroquois plot to drive the English from the Eastern Shore, the Nanticoke leaders were receptive to the idea. Colonel John Ennals noticed the visitors, but thought nothing of it at the time. The Shawnee stayed for about eleven days, then returned to the north.

A couple of weeks later, in early to mid-June, the Nanticokes, Choptanks, Indian River Indians, and Pocomokes quietly left their respective reservations and traveled to a place called Winnasoccum. The exact location of Winnasoccum is unknown, but colonial land records referring to Wimbesoccum (or Wimbasacham, Wimbesacum, etc.) Creek and Neck, and later maps featuring Sockum Creek, suggest that it was about six miles east of Broad Creek Town—or, in today's terms, in the area between Pepper Pond and Trinity United Methodist Church.

Once numerous Indians had assembled at Winnasoccum, a week-long powwow commenced. The details of the plot were explained: In the near future, the Shawnee would secretly return and help the Nanticokes execute a surprise attack on the English settlers during the night. Men, women, and children would be slaughtered, and the attack would continue for as long and as far as possible. Meanwhile, the French, who had been grappling with the English for control of North America for decades, would land on the coast. For the Nanticokes and other tribes, it was to be a desperate, all-or-nothing, last stand against the invaders who had stolen their lands, forced them onto reservations, and destroyed some of the neighboring tribes. In celebration of the plan, some painted their bodies and danced to the sound of beating drums, brandishing tomahawks and firing guns, and a medicine man from Indian River brewed a poison to be dumped into their enemies' water supply.

Had the gathering escaped the notice of the English, the history of the peninsula might have unfolded quite differently. But the white residents of both the Broad Creek area and Dorchester County reported their Indian neighbors' suspicious absence to the authorities in Vienna, and on June 22nd, Colonel Ennals wrote to Colonel Levin Gale, warning that all of the Indians of Dorchester were missing, and that the Broad Creek Indians had left their village to hunt at Winnasoccum. He didn't believe they were hunting, because the old men, women, and children had gone, too, instead of remaining behind to tend the crops. Gale forwarded the letter to Governor Samuel Ogle in Annapolis.

During the next week, several Indians were questioned. Four Choptanks confirmed that the purpose of the gathering at Winnasoccum had been to discuss the plot against the English.

By July 4th, at least twelve Indians had been interrogated. Some claimed that the Broad Creek Indians had told them about a secret log structure on a small island about two or three miles into the swamp, stocked with guns, powder, shot, and many poison-coated, brass-pointed arrows. Meanwhile, the Council of Maryland directed the commander at Vienna to order any Indians in the swamp to surrender their weapons, and to guard the routes out of the swamp to ensure that none escaped to contact the northern tribes.

The Eastern Shore forces succeeded, and on July 12th ten Indians were questioned at a meeting of the Council in Annapolis. The leaders claimed that they had gone to Winnasoccum to hunt and elect an emperor, and denied the existence of any log structure stocked with weapons. Others claimed that they had gone there only because they were told to, and learned of the plot after they arrived.

The Council did not take long to make a decision. On the same day, some of the Indians were warned that they could have been severely punished, and that the English could take all of their lands, but would instead show them mercy. They were released on the condition that they would inform the nearest Justice of the Peace if they saw any "strange Indians." However, their leaders, including Simon Alsechqueck and Captain John of Broad Creek, remained in custody for another twelve days. On July 24th, they were released after signing the most restrictive treaty in the history of the Nanticokes' dealings with the English. They could no longer elect an emperor, and every member of the tribe was forbidden to own a gun without obtaining a license from the governor.

The failure of the plot may have been the last straw for the Nanticokes. Shortly thereafter, an exodus began. In 1744, Simon Alsechqueck and other Nanticoke leaders requested and received permission for the tribe to leave the Eastern Shore and live among the Six Nations of the Iroquois Confederacy. The refugees made their way north, paddling dugout canoes down the Nanticoke River and up the Chesapeake Bay. They joined other displaced tribes along the Susquehanna River for a time, but eventually traveled farther north and settled in French territory. Others moved east, and lived among the Indian River Indians. Their multiracial descendants would found the Nanticoke Indian Association 180 years later.

By 1754, Broad Creek Town was deserted. Any Nanticokes who didn't move away probably lived in cabins on undesirable tracts of land, and were gradually absorbed by the white or black populations through intermarriage. Only stone artifacts and ancient names like Rossakatum, Wimbcsoccom, and Assacatum remained to remind future generations of the first people to call Broad Creek home.

"Sockum" and the Nanticokes of Broad Creek

March 2014

BEGINNING IN 1744, the Nanticokes left their reservations on Chicacoan Creek and Broad Creek, in Dorchester and Sussex Counties, respectively. Most traveled north, up the Chesapeake Bay and Susquehanna River, and lived among the Six Nations of the Iroquois Confederacy before eventually settling in modern-day Ontario. Some moved east, and joined the Indian River Indians. Within a decade, Broad Creek Town was said to be abandoned, and in 1767 the Nanticokes relinquished their claim to the reservation and requested compensation. White settlers bought the land, and eventually the town of Laurel was founded on the site of the old reservation. But did all of the Nanticokes leave the Broad Creek area? If not, where did they live? What happened to them?

The strongest evidence for a Nanticoke presence near Broad Creek during the late 18th and early 19th centuries is the name Sockum, which was both a place name and a surname.

Its meaning is uncertain, though its similarity to sachem, an Algonquian term for chief, is obvious. During the colonial era, the tributary of Broad Creek known today as Gray's Branch was known as Wimbesoccom Creek, and the surrounding area as Wimbesoccom Neck. Several spelling variations can be found in the early records, including Wimbasacham and Winnasoccum. By the 1790s, the name had been shortened to Sockum, and Sockum Creek appeared on maps of the area for the next several decades.

As a surname, Sockum first appears (to the best of my knowledge) in the tax lists for Somerset County, Maryland. In 1756, James and Rachell Sockam were dependents in the household of James Weatherly in Nanticoke Hundred. (Just to be clear, Nanticoke Hundred covered present-day western Sussex. The Delaware hundred of the same name covers a small portion of the same territory.) In 1757, James and Rachell "Scokem" were still living in Nanticoke Hundred, but James was the head of household. Although it's impossible to be certain, I think it's likely that they lived in what is now Little Creek Hundred, the area south of Broad Creek. At that time, the area north and east of Broad Creek was part of Worcester County, not Somerset.

According to the 1785 list of taxables in Dagsborough Hundred (which included the Gumboro area at that time), a James Sockam and a Widow Sockam (meaning the widow of a deceased Sockam) were living in the hundred.

The name next appears in the 1800s. There was a James Socom living in Dagsborough Hundred in 1800, a James Sockam living in Little Creek Hundred in 1810, and a James Soccum living in Dagsborough Hundred in 1820. Was there one James Sockum who moved around? Or were there two or three men with the same name? And was there a connection to the James Sockum documented in 1756 and 1757?

In 1830, a free "negro" named William Sockum was living in Broad Creek Hundred with his wife and daughter. However, it's important to remember that Indians were considered "colored" or "mulattoes" in 19th-century Delaware. Only after a long struggle did the multiracial descendants of the Nanticokes and Indian River Indians win recognition and respect as the Nanticoke Indians. William Sockum could have been 100% black, and I don't deny that he probably had African ancestors—otherwise he would have been labeled a mulatto—but I suspect he also had Nanticoke ancestors.

In 1840, Elisha Sockom, a free "colored" man, was living in Dagsborough Hundred with his wife and four children. I'm not sure if he was the same Elisha Sockum who died in Philadelphia in 1881; according to his death certificate, he was born about 1794 in Sussex County, Delaware. Another free "colored" man named S. Souckum was living in Philadelphia in 1840; he was the first Sockum outside of Sussex County to be counted in the census, which supports the theory that Sockum was and is a Nanticoke name.

By 1850, there were two distinct Sockum families living in Sussex County. Isaac Sockum, a 40-year-old mulatto, was living in Broadkill Hundred, near Milton, with his wife and two daughters. The area around his farm became known as Sockumtown. One of his sons later reported that he had been told that Sockum was an Indian name, and that the family was descended from a white man and an Indian chief's daughter. Meanwhile, Levin Sockum, a 40-year-old mulatto whose relationship to Isaac Sockum is unclear, was living in Indian River Hundred with his wife and ten children. Locals called the area on the north shore of Indian River "Sockum" or "Down Sockum," supposedly because numerous Sockums lived there, but only Levin and his immediate family were counted in the 1850 and 1860 censuses. Levin was a storekeeper. In

1855, he was convicted of illegally selling ammunition to a so-called mulatto of Indian descent. The following year, he was convicted of illegally possessing a firearm, despite the fact that he did not consider himself to be a mulatto and claimed Indian ancestry. Following the humiliating trials, the family left the area. Most of them settled in New Jersey, where they were recognized as Indians, and changed their last name to Sockume. Some moved to San Francisco. There were also Sockums living in Philadelphia and New York in 1860.

In conclusion (for now), census records indicate an eastward migration of the name Sockum between 1756 and 1840. As both a place name and a surname, it first appears in the Broad Creek area. Later it appears near Indian River and the town of Milton. This doesn't prove that all (or any) of the Sockums were descended from Nanticokes of the Broad Creek reservation, but I think that's the best explanation. Maybe the story old Isaac Sockum told his children was true. Maybe a white man married the daughter of one of the last local chiefs of the Nanticoke people. Maybe their descendants were wrongly classified as mulattoes and persons of color, but handed down the story of their roots, generation after generation, even as they migrated across Sussex County and eventually moved to other states.

James Sockam of Dagsborough Hundred

August 2014

A few months ago I wrote an article entitled "'Sockum' and the Nanticokes of Broad Creek," which explains why I believe the name Sockum, as both a surname and place-name, followed Nanticoke refugees as they drifted across the Eastern Shore between 1744 and 1850.

When researching the subject, I missed at least one fact, which I just noticed yesterday. It might not be all that important, but every little bit of information helps.

Scharf's *History of Delaware* features a list of taxables in Dagsborough Hundred in 1785. This list proves that a James Sockam and a Widow Sockam (meaning the widow of a deceased Sockam) were living in the hundred at that time, which included the area later known as Gumborough Hundred. Interestingly, there was a James Sockam living in Nanticoke Hundred, Somerset County (probably in what would become Little Creek Hundred, Sussex County, following the resolution of the boundary dispute) in the 1750s. There was also a James Sockum living in Sussex County in the early 1800s. Without more information, it's impossible to know how many Jameses we're dealing with, but it seems likely that there were at least two or three generations of men named James Sockum (or Sockam, Soccom, etc.).

It should be remembered that just as there were Nanticoke reservations along Chicacoan Creek and Broad Creek, there was a thousand-acre "Indian River Indian" reservation located near a tributary of Indian River known today as Irons Branch. Injun Town Road, located in Dagsboro Hundred, south of Millsboro, seems to trace the southern boundary of this tract. The Indian River Indians sold sections of the reservation in the 1730s and early 1740s, with the final tract being sold in late 1743. Presumably some of them migrated north with the Nanticokes, and presumably some of them stayed in the area, eventually moving to the north shore of Indian River. It's possible that the James Sockam of 1785 was living with or near descendants of the Indian River Indians in the neighborhood of their old reservation.

The Sockum Family: Further Research

August 2016

In March of 2014 I wrote an article entitled "Sockum and the Nanticokes of Broad Creek," which summarized genealogical and historical data connecting the Sockum family to the Nanticoke Indians who lived around Broad Creek in the 18th century. The information raised more questions than it answered; although many Sockums appeared in early records—even as early as 1756—it's difficult to connect them to each other.

Although I haven't uncovered any major new information or indisputable evidence of a Sockum-Nanticoke connection, with the annual Nanticoke Indian Powwow coming up in a few weeks, now is a perfect time to offer a somewhat tentative interpretation of some of the early Sockum information which might help us to better understand this family's history. I want to make it clear that I'm engaging in speculation here—very informed speculation, based on primary sources like census and tax records—but speculation nonetheless.

I. James & Rachel Sockam, 1756 – 1757, near Rewastico Creek

The story begins with James Sockam and his wife, Rachel, who were living in the household of James Weatherly in Nanticoke Hundred, Somerset County, Maryland, in 1756. The following year, they had their own household in the same hundred. Lest today's reader wrongly assume that this location was in today's Somerset County, a word of explanation is in order. At that time, there was no Wicomico County, and Somerset and Worcester Counties included more than half of today's Sussex County, Delaware. Nanticoke Hundred was the area between the Nanticoke and Wicomico Rivers, roughly. Somerset stretched northward along the west side of Stage Road to the site of present-day Laurel on Broad Creek.

Although the fairly large Nanticoke Hundred included (in today's terms) Quantico, Hebron, parts of Salisbury, Delmar, and half of Laurel, land records pertaining to James Weatherly and other members of the Weatherly family help us to narrow it down. In 1716, a 136-acre tract of land named Weatherles Marshes was described as "lying and being in Somerset County on the southernmost side of Nanticoak River and on ye north side of Rowasticoe Creek…" The tract was patented to James and William Weatherly in 1728. In 1755, a 75-acre tract named Weatherly's Lot was surveyed for James Weatherly, and was described as "Begining at a Marked Read Oak standing on the North side of Rewastico Creek back in the woods and on the East side of the main Road that leads from Rewastico Mill to Barren Creek Mill…" Other surveys pertaining to the Weatherly family point at the same general area: East of the

Nanticoke, north of Rewastico Creek, and south of Barren Creek, roughly in the neighborhood of Hebron.

The record for 1757 tells us little more. James "Scokem" was now a head of household, but hadn't moved far; James Weatherly's household number was 163, while Sockam's was 167. No household members other than Rachel are listed, but they wouldn't have been unless they were at least 15 years old, so the couple may have had children.

The will of James Weatherly, Sr., dated 1761, mentions several slaves by their first names, as well as oddly referring to Joseph Weatherly as his "friend," but does not mention the Sockams or offer any clues as to why they were dependents in his household just five years earlier. The place name Cedar Landing appears in the will a couple of times.

So it seems that I was wrong two years ago when I stated that James and Rachel Sockam probably lived in what is now Little Creek Hundred, Sussex County, Delaware. Between 1756 and 1757, at least, they lived near Rewastico Creek. The difference isn't major—the two neighborhoods are only separated by a few miles, maybe a dozen, probably fewer than twenty—and doesn't affect the theory that James Sockam might have been a Nanticoke Indian, since the territory in question was still Nanticoke territory, and wasn't far from Chicacoan Town. However, it was a bit far from Wimbesoccom Creek, later known as Sockum Creek. I still believe that there must be a connection between this Nanticoke Indian place-name and the Sockum surname, but obviously the connection is a mystery at this point, and the fact that the earliest known Sockum didn't live near Wimbesoccom raises even more questions.

II. Sockums in Dagsborough Hundred, 1770s – 1800

James—or possibly a son named James—next appears in "Dagsberry" Hundred in 1777, along with an Isaac Sockom. Both were considered colored. James appears in records throughout the 1780s and 1790s, always in Dagsborough Hundred. In 1784, a "widow Sockam" is mentioned. In 1795–1796, a Lowder or Loweder Sockum was taxed, also in Dagsborough Hundred. At that time, the hundred included the area east of Broad Creek, south of Indian River, and west of Vine Creek, including part of the future Gumborough Hundred. Interestingly, it also included the site of the old "Indian River Indian" reservation known as Askesky. The reservation lands were no longer owned by Indians in 1777, but it's certainly possible that remnants of the local Indian tribes still lived nearby—and the Sockums in question may have been some of them.

These Indians (or part Indians) had consciously chosen to stay behind when most of the Nanticokes migrated north a few decades earlier. Why? We can only speculate. Maybe they had already mixed with whites and/or blacks and weren't really considered part of the tribe. Maybe they preferred to adopt European culture, even if that meant forsaking much of their heritage and living as mulattoes. Maybe they just couldn't bear to leave their homeland.

There is no proof that James Sockam was a Nanticoke Indian, or even part Indian. However, he certainly wasn't white. My personal theory at this time is that he was at least part Nanticoke, probably with white and/or black blood, making him "colored" in the eyes of his white neighbors. His colored descendants—whether considered mulattoes or Negroes—would have naturally been more likely to marry blacks than whites due to the attitude of the times. Yet they also would have been likely to preserve stories of Indian ancestry if, in fact, they had any. If this was the case, then we should expect later Sockums to remember that heritage—which is exactly what happened in at least two branches of the family (see Section III).

The gap between 1757 and 1777 might have something to do with the resolution of the boundary dispute between Maryland and Pennsylvania. A resident of the Dagsborough Hundred area prior to 1775 or thereabouts wouldn't have appeared in any Sussex County records, since the territory was still claimed by Worcester County, Maryland.

III. Sockums in Sussex County, 1800 – 1820s

The name James Sockum (with spelling variations) appears in census records for 1800, 1810, and 1820:

> 1800: James Socom, Dagsborough Hundred, 4 free persons in household

> 1810: James Sockem, Little Creek Hundred, 8 free persons in household

> 1820: James Soccomm (or Soccaum; spelling unclear), Dagsborough Hundred, 2 foreigners not naturalized

These records raise more questions than they answer. Although each record indicates that the entire household was non-white, the connection to Little Creek Hundred is a bit confusing. It's also unclear whether we're dealing with one man named James Sockum, or more. With records spanning 1756 through 1820—a period of 64 years—it seems certain that there were at least two. But was the James Sockam living in Dagsborough Hundred in 1820 the same man who was living there in 1777? Probably, but we can't be certain.

The Little Creek Hundred record might be explained by the will of Levin Thompson, dated 1804 (with additions as late as 1810). Thompson was a free black man who settled in Little Creek Hundred in the 1790s. He became rather wealthy and is an important figure in the history of the Laurel area, and may also be important in the history of the Sockum family. In 1801, Thompson was taxed in Dagsborough Hundred (where he also owned land), and apparently he had purchased 80 acres from James Sockam, though I've yet to find the deed. In his will, he left "the place where James Sockam formerly lived" to his son, "Clemmon." It's not entirely clear whether he was referring to land in Little Creek Hundred or Dagsborough Hundred. However, in 1817, Clement Thompson sold Levi Hopkins an 89-acre parcel of land in Dagsborough Hundred, which was described as "Beginning at a marked white oak standing on the north side of Shelah's Branch between James Sockums and Ezekiel [Mearres?]…" Perhaps this parcel included the 80 acres his father had purchased from James Sockum years earlier. Assuming that Shelah's Branch was an early name for Shoals or Shields Branch, the location was tantalizingly close to the site of the old Indian reservation, as well as Wimbesoccom Neck.

My personal theory at this time is that the records from 1777 through 1820 all referred to the same man, who may have been the son of the James Sockam who lived near Rewastico Creek in the 1750s. This second James Sockam/Sockum was considered colored, probably had at least six children, and probably died in the 1820s.

IV. Sockums in Sussex County, 1820s – 1880s

Between 1821 and 1850, four Sockum households were established in Sussex County, headed by men close enough in age to have been brothers, although there is no proof of that. In fact, their relationship to each other is unknown. But, since I'm speculating, let's consider the possibility that all four were James Sockam's sons.

William Sockum was born between 1795 and 1806. In 1830, he was a "Negro" head of household in Broad Creek Hundred (which included the future Gumborough Hundred at that time) with a wife and a daughter under the age of 10. He might have moved away and died in Philadelphia in 1846; further research is needed.

Levin Sockum was born in 1807, and was a head of household in Indian River Hundred by 1840. He had many children, and is the best-known Sockum for being convicted of selling ammunition and gunpowder to a mulatto in the 1850s, despite the buyer's claim to be an Indian rather than a mulatto. The story of the trial has been told in many sources, notably *Delaware's Forgotten Folk* by C. A. Weslager, so I won't go into further detail here. His neighborhood was nicknamed Sockum or Down Sockum. Levin moved to New Jersey in the early 1860s, changed the family name to Sockume, and died in 1864. Levin's branch of the family insisted that they were Indians, not mulattoes or Negroes.

Elisha Sockom was born between 1805 and 1816, and was a head of household in Dagsborough Hundred in 1840. He was described as colored, and had three or four children at the time. He appears to have moved to Camden County, New Jersey, where records suggest that he may have been a few years older. An 1880 census record and his death certificate state that he was born in 1794.

Levin Sockum and wife Eunice Ridgeway. It is likely that Levin's grandfather was a Nanticoke Indian who stayed behind when the tribe moved north between the 1740s and 1760s.

Isaac Sockum was born circa 1811, and was a head of household in Broadkill Hundred by 1850. He was described as a mulatto. He and his wife, Louise or Louisa Sammons, had several children. Interestingly, one son was named James. Another, Stephen, is mentioned in *Delaware's Forgotten Folk*, and reported that Isaac had claimed that the family was descended from a white man who married an Indian chief's daughter. Isaac died in Milton in 1894 at the age of 83. At one time the site of his farm was known as Sockumtown.

Another Sockum of unknown origin from this period is a 41-year-old Stephen Sockum who died in 1850 and was buried in the Bethel Colored Burial Ground in Philadelphia, indicating that the Sockum family's connection to Philadelphia and/or Camden County, New Jersey, existed before Levin moved there in the 1860s.

Yet another person of interest is Ann Sockam, who married Josiah Miller in Kent County, Delaware, in 1849. Although I haven't done any research on this couple, it's worth noting that Cheswold, Kent County, was (and is, to an extent) the home of a multiracial community of so-called Moors, which is known to have been connected to the similar community in Sussex County which founded the Nanticoke Indian Association. Additionally, there was a neighborhood named Sockum near Felton in the mid-19th century.

Of course, we can't be certain that any of these individuals were siblings, but it seems likely that they were closely related. Names like James (for example, Levin's son Levin James Sockum), Isaac, and Stephen appear often enough for a blood connection to be logical. So why did they all live so far apart? This is a mystery, especially since my theory holds that all had roots in Dagsborough Hundred, and in the original Nanticoke territory prior to that. One possibility which would require quite a bit of research to investigate is that the men married into other multiracial families living in smaller "Moor" communities which preceded the larger and better-known communities in Indian River Hundred and Cheswold. Isaac's settlement in Broadkill Hundred may have had more to do with job opportunities; as a ship's carpenter (in 1880), there were only so many places to work.

V. Thoughts on the Sockum Family's Indian Heritage

The fact that both Levin and Isaac Sockum—who may or may not have been brothers—told their children stories about Indian heritage suggests that there was truth behind those stories. *If* they were brothers, and *if* their father was James Sockam of Dagsborough Hundred, and *if* his father was James Sockam of Rewastico Creek, then they were separated from the Nanticoke era—i.e., the reservations at Chicacoan and

Broad Creek, and the Wimbesoccom event, and the exodus beginning in the late 1740s—by only a couple of generations. They thought of their Indian heritage the way that today's millennials think of the Great Depression; they hadn't experienced it directly, but they had learned about it from people who had; it was much more than some distant myth.

The specific details of that heritage, of course, are very unclear. One problem with Isaac Sockum's claim that a white man married the daughter of an Indian chief is that it doesn't explain the surname; if Sockum is a Nanticoke name, then it's highly unlikely that an Englishman would have adopted it or passed it on to his heirs. It's more likely that an Englishman fathered illegitimate children with an Indian woman, and they wound up with an Indian surname. Or, a freed black slave with no surname married an Indian woman, and adopted an Indian name.

Another problem, though it's a very minor one, is that the name Sockum isn't connected to any known Indian individual in any historical sources. Maryland records include a number of 18th-century Nanticoke surnames, such as Asquash, Coursey, and Puckum, but neither Sockum nor any similar term appears in those records (of course, Sockum and Puckum are somewhat similar, but no link between the two has been found). However, since Wimbesoccom Creek was certainly a Nanticoke name, and it was later shortened to Sockum Creek, I think it's safe to assume that the surname was also of Nanticoke origin.

It's interesting—but possibly a meaningless coincidence—that Sockum sounds similar to the Algonquin term *sachem*, which means chief or emperor, and that when the Nanticokes and other tribes held their famous powwow at Wimbesoccom in 1742, they claimed that they had gone there to elect an emperor. Could it be that the site was traditionally used by the tribe to meet and choose emperors? I tend to doubt it (I think the tribes met there in 1742 because it was conveniently located between the reservations at Broad Creek and Askesky, and was on the outskirts of the swamp), but I mention the possibility for the sake of thoroughness.

VI. Avenues for Further Research

The subject of the roots of the Sockum family is far from closed, and there are a number points which deserve further research, such as:

> 1. The exact location of James Weatherly's plantation near Rewastico Creek, and an explanation for why James and Rachel Sockam were living in his household in 1756. There is at least one reference to a tract of land named Sockum located in this general area; finding more information about it could be helpful.
>
> 2. The meaning of Wimbesoccom and Sockum in the Nanticoke language. Although Nanticoke is considered a dead language, clues might be found in other Algonquin languages. These names were not just random combinations of sounds; they meant something to the people who used them in and prior to the 1750s.
>
> 3. The presence of Sockums in New Jersey and/or Philadelphia in the early to mid-19th century. It seems clear that they moved there from Sussex County, but when? And why?
>
> 4. The presence of Sockums in Kent County, Delaware,

as well as the fact that there was a neighborhood named Sockum near Felton. When did the name begin to appear in records?

5. More information on William Sockum and Elisha Sockom, who may have been part of the early migration to New Jersey and/or Philadelphia.

6. More information on the spouses of the Sockums, and their ancestry.

Regua, Rigware, Ridgeway: The Evolution of a Mysterious Surname

March 2017

During the last couple of years I've written several articles about the Sockum family, notable for their unique surname and probable connection to the Nanticoke Indians. It's a bit easier to research an unusual name like Sockum than others that are associated with the Nanticokes and Moors, such as Clark and Johnson.

The name Ridgeway might seem, at first glance, to be similarly mainstream, but a closer look at the Ridgeway family reveals that their name wasn't originally Ridgeway, and they can be traced to a specific neighborhood in Sussex County. Considering their association with one of the oldest legends about the Moors' origins, they are certainly deserving of more attention than they've received.

Notable Ridgeways include Eunice Ridgeway (1813 – 1896), the wife of Levin Sockum; and Cornelius Ridgeway, who was described as the "patriarch" of the Cheswold Moors in 1895, and who related a version of the legend in question.

Though there are a number of versions of what C. A. Weslager later dubbed the Romantic Legend, dating back to the 1850s but primarily recorded in the 1890s, many of the details are consistent. Rather than quote or summarize each version individually, I'll list the core points:

- A white woman settled in or near Angola Neck, southwest of Lewes and in Indian River Hundred, roughly fifteen to twenty years before the American Revolution (i.e., 1756 – 1761).

- She was either Irish or Spanish, or, in one version, Irish with a claim to an estate in Spain.

- Her name was Regua, Señorita Requa, or Miss Reegan.

- She purchased some newly arrived slaves in Lewes, one of whom was very handsome. According to most versions, he could speak Spanish, and told her he was a Spanish and/or Moorish prince who had been sold into slavery. In one version, his name was Requa.

- The two married and produced mixed descendants who were scorned by the local whites, yet did not wish to marry the local blacks, so they either intermarried amongst themselves or married Indians. Their descendants in Indian River Hundred were numerous. Red hair is often mentioned.

- The name Regua (or Requa, etc.) evolved into the surname Ridgeway.

The facts are less dramatic, though they don't disprove any of the plot points listed above, and are remarkably compatible with them.

John Regua, Indian River Hundred, 1740s – 1790s?

A mulatto whose name was recorded as John Rigway, John Regua, John Rigwaugh, John Rigwaw, and John Rigware, among other similar spellings, was living in Indian River Hundred as early as the 1740s. His daughters were baptized at St. George's in 1748, and he purchased nearly 300 acres of land near Swan Creek from Cord Hazzard between 1753 and 1754. Variations of his name appear on tax lists throughout the following decades, and in my opinion, most of these creative spellings suggest that the name was not pronounced like the English surname Ridgeway. It seems more likely that the writers were struggling to spell a name which was unfamiliar, and probably foreign.

Although Regua is a rather obscure term, it could very well be Portuguese. Peso de Régua (or Pezo de Regoa) is a city in northern Portugal, and similar names can be found in Spain and in the Pacific. It should perhaps be noted here that another surname suspected to be of Portuguese or Spanish origin, Driggas or Driggers (possibly derived from Rodrigues or Rodriguez), appears in Indian River Hundred as early as 1770.

Little is known of John's immediate family, and it's difficult to connect the dots between him and later generations with certainty, but it's likely that he had sons named William and Isaac, who, like him, appear in early tax lists for Indian River Hundred, as well as the records of St. George's. In July 1785, William and Jane Riguway baptized a child who had been born nearly a year earlier, and just a few weeks later, Isaac and

Lydia Riguway baptized a daughter named Allender. Isaac's fate is unknown, but William appears in a number of records including the 1820 census (which vaguely described him as being 45 or older), and died before November 1826.

The Rigware family in Indian River Hundred, 1810 – 1840s

Census records allow us to identify several Rigware households in Indian River Hundred between 1810 and 1840, headed by:

1. William Rigware, Sr., enumerated in 1820 and most likely the same man who was a taxable as early as 1774, and who is assumed to be John Regua's eldest son. Interestingly, William's household included one female slave who was 45 or older in 1820.

2. Peter Rigware, age unknown, enumerated in 1810.

3. John Rigware, enumerated in 1810 and 1820 with a birthdate range of 1776 – 1794. He is most likely the same man who appears in the 1830 census as John Rigway, aged 55 – 99, with a birthdate range of 1731–1775, and again in the 1850 census as 73-year-old John Ridgeway, living in the household of Nathaniel Clark in Lewis and Rehoboth Hundred. Comparison of these slightly conflicting records suggests that he was born circa 1776.

4. Simon Rigware, enumerated in 1820 and 1840, with a birthdate range of 1776 – 1785. In 1840, his name was given as "Simon Rigware alias Jack."

5. Jacob Rigware, enumerated in 1820 with a birthdate range of 1776 – 1794. In 1850, a 60-year-old Jacob Ridgway was living in the household of John and Hetty Harmon in Broadkill Hundred. If they are the same man, then Jacob was born circa 1790.

With the exception of the enigmatic female slave living in William Rigware's household in 1820 (who may very well have been a family member), all of these men and their family members were described as free colored persons or mulattoes. Although researchers using resources like Ancestry.com will find transcribed spellings like Rigwars and Rigwan, a closer look at the handwritten records suggested that the correct spelling is, indeed, Rigware. It should be noted that during this period, the family remained concentrated in Indian River Hundred.

Rigware, Ridgway, and Ridgeway in 1850

The 1850 U.S. Federal Census is notable for the amount of information it provides. Previously, only heads of household were named, and the members of the household were vaguely listed by gender and age ranges. In 1850 (and in every census since), each member of the household was identified by name and age. When it comes to the Rigware family, the 1850 census provides evidence for two important trends. First, they had begun to migrate northward, appearing in Lewes and Rehoboth Hundred, Broadkill Hundred, and Cedar Creek Hundred. Second, the name had been changed to Ridgway in certain instances.

Confusingly, the 1850 census also includes a number of Ridgeways who might or might not be related to the Rigwares.

Connections to both New Jersey and Indiana are noted, which ought to interest anyone researching Nanticoke genealogy. However, I'll ignore these households for the moment and focus on those which can reasonably be assumed to be related to the Rigwares of Indian River Hundred.

As was mentioned previously, John Ridgway, a 73-year-old mulatto, was living in the household of Nathaniel Clark in Lewes and Rehoboth Hundred. The name Clark, of course, has been associated with the Nanticoke Indian Association since its beginnings, and it was Lydia Clark who first recited a version of the Romantic Legend in 1855. Nathaniel's wife was named Unicey, and they also had a daughter named Unicey, which might suggest some connection to Eunice Ridgeway, who was living with her husband, Levin Sockum, in Indian River Hundred at the time. It's possible that the elder Unicey was John's daughter, in which case her maiden name would have been Rigware or Ridgway. Some relationship between all of these individuals seems likely.

Another John Ridgway was living in Broadkill Hundred at the time, though this one was 35. His wife, Sophia, was 20, while a third member of the household, 18-year-old Matilda Ridgway, may have been a younger sister.

Also in Broadkill Hundred was the household of John Harmon, who was 25. The only other members were his wife, Hetty, who was 20, and Jacob Ridgway, 60.

Moving northward, we come to the household of William Rigware, age 46, in Cedar Creek Hundred. He is assumed to have been the son of William Rigware, Sr., who lived in Indian River Hundred. William is notable for three reasons:

> 1. He was the father of Cornelius Ridgeway, who was later described as the patriarch of the Cheswold Moors, and who recalled a version of the Romantic Legend.

2. He continued to migrate northward between 1850 and 1860; when one considers his assumed residence in Indian River Hundred between his birth around 1804 and his father's death in 1826, he is practically a direct link between the Indian River and Cheswold communities.

3. By 1860, he, too, had changed his surname to Ridgeway.

Another person of interest in the 1850 census is a mulatto named Tilman (or Tilghman) Jack, who was living in Dover Hundred with his wife and six children. By 1870, he had become Tilghman Ridway and was living in Northwest Fork Hundred, near Seaford; by 1880, Tilghman Ridgeway and family were back in Dover. It should be remembered that Simon Rigware of Indian River Hundred was called "Simon Rigware alias Jack" in 1840. The significance of the Jack name is unclear.

The Ridgeway family in Kent County, 1850s – 1890s

By 1860, William Rigware had become William Ridgeway, and had moved his family to Duck Creek Hundred. Personally, I believe the change from Rigware to Ridgeway was deliberate. The former spelling, which followed older spellings like Rigwaugh and Regua, was used consistently for decades. I find it hard to believe that multiple individuals previously known as Rigwares suddenly became Ridgways or Ridgeways in 1850 without having decided to. It was not long after this that Levin Sockum's family changed both the spelling and pronunciation of their surname to Sockume (*sock-yoom*). It's possible that some of the multiracial families who claimed Indian ancestry changed their names during this period in a subtle attempt to improve their social status. Rigware was a mulatto name, Ridgeway was a white name—or so they may have reasoned. This is not to say that they were attempting to claim to be white; they continued to be described as mulattoes, and sometimes as blacks. Yet Weslager wrote of some of the Cheswold Moors successfully "passing" for white and moving away.

Cornelius Ridgeway—who was probably the great-grandson of John Regua—was talking about his own family's history when he told a journalist about the legend of Señorita Requa in 1895, and had himself been a Rigware as a young boy.

Conclusion

Although there is no evidence that the Ridgeway family associated with the Nanticokes and Moors is descended from a white woman who married a handsome slave on her plantation in the Angola area in the 1750s, it's a matter of fact that a free mulatto named John Regua bought a considerable amount of land in the right area during the right time period, and his descendants lived in Indian River Hundred for nearly a century before they began to migrate northward, and their surname evolved into Rigware by the late 18th century and Ridgeway by the mid-19th century. These facts are delightfully compatible with the core points of the Romantic Legend.

I should note at this point that there is no obvious connection to the historical Nanticoke Indians who lived along the Nanticoke River. I've called Ridgeway a Nanticoke surname because it is associated with the modern Nanticoke Indian Association and related groups in Kent County and New Jersey.

This article might have raised more questions than it has answered. Who was John Regua? Where did he come from? Where did he come by what seems to be a Portuguese name? Is it a coincidence that men named Driggas were among his neighbors, and Angola Neck was named after a major Portuguese colony?

Other surnames with a possible Portuguese or Spanish connection are found throughout the colonial records of the peninsula, such as Gonsolvos (Gonçalves), Francisco, and Dias. Some of them were associated with the Cheswold Moors.

When one considers these curious facts, the legends of the Nanticokes and Moors—including not only the Romantic Legend, but also tales involving shipwrecked pirates—begin to sound surprisingly plausible.

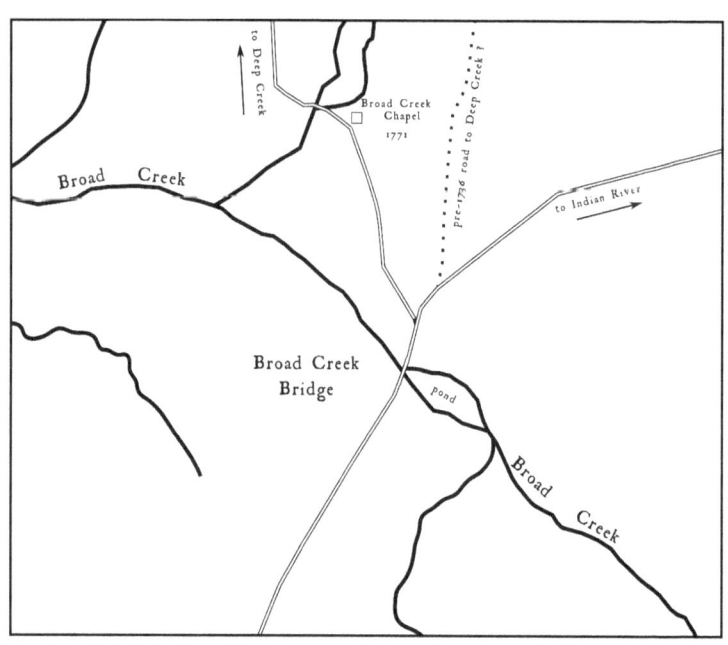

Broad Creek Bridge and the Old Forge

September 2019

One of the lesser-known chapters in the history of the Laurel area concerns a vanished community which was located in the wooded area south of Sandy Fork and the American Legion home, commonly called Old Forge. The mysterious site was an important one in the 18th and 19th centuries, featuring a bridge over Broad Creek for travelers using the original stage road. The Pomeroy & Beers Atlas of 1868 depicts a sawmill, gristmill, store, and several houses clustered around the bridge. There was also an African Methodist Episcopal church on the south side of the creek at that time, but it does not appear on the map. In the early years of the 20th century, "Old Forge Camp" was described as the largest "colored" campmeeting in Sussex County. Today, the forge, mills, houses, church, campground, bridge, and even the road are long gone.

Old Forge has received little attention from historians, probably because the name doesn't appear in early records.

Local journalist Orlando V. Wootten wrote two fascinating articles about Old Forge for the *Daily Times* and *The Archeolog* in 1968 and 1975, respectively, based on his own visits to the site as well as information from Carmel Moore. Both were accompanied by striking photos of abandoned millstones and other features. The second article was reprinted in *The History of Nineteenth Century Laurel* in 1983. Wootten lamented the absence of "documentary evidence or primary sources of historical information on Old Forge," despite the fact that Scharf's *History of Delaware* mentioned that the forge and mills had been built "many years before" 1807, when they were owned by Josiah Polk.

But the reason for Old Forge's apparent absence from early records is simple: The community wasn't called Old Forge back then. It was called Broad Creek Bridge.

Possibly the earliest references to Broad Creek Bridge were made in 1723, when the area was part of Nanticoke Hundred in Somerset County, Maryland:

"Thomas Gordan appointed Overseer of the roads in Nanticoak hundred from Broad Creek bridge to the Cows bridge at the head of the Indian river..."

"Henry Friggs appointed Overseer of the roads in the afsd hundred from Broad Creek to Gravelly Branch..."

A similar reference appears the following year:

"Ordered that James Bowcher be overseer of the road from Broad Creek bridge halfe way to the Cow bridge it being the halfe of Wm. Burtons Limmitts from the Cow Bridge..."

Friggs is probably the same man called Henry Freaks in 1711, who was awarded 3,000 pounds of tobacco in damages due to the creation of the Nanticoke reservation known as Broad Creek Town. James Bouger was another early landowner.

The bridge was also used as a landmark in surveys of nearby tracts of land. In 1726, "Cypress Swamp" was surveyed for Robert Givans, and described as beginning at a red oak on the northeast side of the creek, "about a mile & halfe above ye Bridge…" Three years later, the first bounder of "Givans Lot" was a cypress tree a mere two poles (approximately 33 feet) below the bridge. Another survey for Givans mentions a cart road leading eastward from the bridge to a swamp; this road might have been the basis of part of today's Route 24. Givans owned several hundred acres of land around Broad Creek Bridge, as well as lands along Deep Creek to the north.

A noteworthy reference appears in 1736, when Paris Chipman petitioned for permission to clear a new road, at his own expense, between Broad Creek Bridge and Chipman's mill dam. Evidently Chipman had built a sawmill downstream of a wading place where the old road crossed a branch, causing the wading place to become impassable. It is likely that this record describes the creation of Chipman's Pond, and that the new pond flooded the old road and wading place.

Another interesting reference appears in 1747, when Presbyterian minister Rev. Charles Tenant mentioned Broad Creek Bridge in a list of places for "public service and preaching…" This is significant, because the early religious history of Broad Creek is a bit mysterious. In the 1880s, Scharf's contributor Rev. Benjamin Douglass suggested that Christ Church, built in 1771, replaced an earlier structure, vaguely citing local tradition.

Additionally, it is known that a Presbyterian church was built along the same branch sometime prior to the Revolution, during which it was burned. Tenant's mention of Broad Creek Bridge is also significant because he seems to be using the name to refer to the community located around the bridge, as opposed to earlier records which seem to use the name to refer to the literal bridge. However, although his list specifically mentions meeting houses at other locations, it does not actually say that there was one at Broad Creek Bridge. The history of the Broad Creek Presbyterians between the 1740s and 1780s deserves further research.

The 1750s saw several surveys for Joseph Marshall which mention Broad Creek Bridge, roads, and other features. Perhaps the most important is a 1755 resurvey of a tract including land formerly owned by Robert Givans, and excluding land which had been "taken away by water." The new 114-acre tract was called Saw Mill Lot. Although the document does not say whether there was already a sawmill there, the reference to encroaching water suggests that the creek had already been dammed to create a mill pond. This could have occurred as early as the late 1720s or early 1730s, under Robert Givans. In any case, it is clear that Saw Mill Lot surrounded the section of Broad Creek which would later be known as Old Forge Pond.

In 1770, the Maryland legislature authorized the purchase of "a Lott of Ground at or near Broad Creek Bridge in [Stepney] Parish and Erecting and Building thereon a Chapel of Ease to the said Parish," resulting in the construction of Broad Creek Chapel between 1771 and 1772. Tradition holds that the iron nails, hinges, etc., used in the structure were produced at the nearby forge. It's not clear why the site at Chipman's Pond, about a mile north of Broad Creek Bridge, was chosen, but the decision seems to support the theory that the name Broad Creek Bridge was used to refer to the entire community at that time.

By 1807, as mentioned previously, Josiah Polk owned

the forge, gristmill, and sawmill at the site. When he died—probably in the late 1830s—ownership passed to his brother, John, although the old forge was abandoned. The mills were called the Polk Mills during this period, even after they were sold to the Chipman family. They were operated during most of the 19th century, changing hands several times.

Both the mills and the bridge were mentioned in 1848, when James Horsey donated a half-acre parcel on the south side of the creek to a group of free blacks led by Samson Matthews. The church they founded would be known as Old Forge A.M.E., though the name does not appear in the deed. The congregation hosted an annual campmeeting beginning in 1855. The church was closed in 1909, but sister church Mt. Pisgah continued to hold campmeetings for several years. In The Churches of Delaware, published in 1947, Zebley stated that nothing survived to mark the site. The history of this church and campmeeting will be explored in greater detail in a future article.

The community at Broad Creek Bridge can be considered a direct ancestor of the town of Laurel, and it is to be hoped that we will be able to learn more about its story, from its mysterious beginnings in the colonial era until its seemingly rapid abandonment in the late 19th and early 20th centuries. Specifics about the Old Forge, in particular, are elusive. The search continues.

Jarrett Willey, Innholder at Broad Creek

November 2019

In March of 1737, a man named Jarrett Willey petitioned the Somerset County Court for permission to keep "an Ordinary or house of Entertainment at his house at broad Creek in Somerset County for the Use and Conveniency of the Inhabitants Travellers and Strangers. . ." The Court granted his request, under the condition that he would pay a yearly fee of fifty shillings, and keep an orderly establishment. Tippling, gaming, and "disorders or other Irregularities" were not to be tolerated. Local planters Robert Givans and Allen Gray provided security; they would be fined if Willey failed to follow the rules.

Technically, an ordinary was a tavern or restaurant, but in this part of the colonies, the term was also used to refer to inns. In this case, the Court record specifically calls Willey an "Inholder"—that is, an innholder or innkeeper. His ordinary would have been one of the most important places at Broad

Creek at the time; a place for travelers to stay overnight, and for locals to gather.

Willey's name appears on the Somerset County tax lists for 1737 – 1740, but the spelling is inconsistent. For example, in 1740, it was Jerad Willy. Also in 1740, he petitioned the Court again; this record is nearly identical to the one from 1737, with Jonathan Shockley and Paris Chipman providing security.

The exact location of Willey's establishment is unclear, but it seems to have been located at or near the community known as Broad Creek Bridge, near today's Sandy Fork. In 1741, some of the residents of the easternmost reaches of Broad Creek petitioned for the creation of a new road leading from "Jarrad Wiley on broad Creek" into Wimbesocom Neck, a distance of several miles. This road may have been the basis of parts of today's Route 24.

Willey makes another appearance, this time in the land records, in 1742. His first name is spelled Garrett. A triangular 50-acre tract was surveyed for him and described as being in the fork of two roads leading from Broad Creek Bridge to the Wicomico River and Wicomico forest, respectively. This certainly sounds like a good location for an ordinary, but it's not clear how Willey used his new tract of land, which was patented to him in 1746.

The handful of references to Jarrett Willey, innholder at Broad Creek, offer us a better understanding of the early Broad Creek Bridge community, which we still know so little about.

Laurel's Forgotten House of Worship?

August 2014

OLD CHRIST CHURCH is probably Laurel's best-kept secret. The locals know all about it, but the hordes of vacationers traveling up and down Route 13 have no idea that they're within walking distance of a beautiful wooden chapel that has changed little since it was erected before the American Revolution. Located next to Chipman's Pond, at a quiet wooded corner a mile or so east of the highway, the church and its ancient graveyard have lingered for generations, virtually untouched by time. And this is not one of those historical sites surrounded by fences and "keep out" signs; the public is invited into the magnificent structure several times a year for special services. I attended one such service this morning, and thoroughly enjoyed the sensation of stepping into the past.

The church's history is well-documented. It was built by Robert Houston, a wealthy shipbuilder and Presbyterian, between 1771 and 1772, and was originally known as Broad

Creek Chapel. Houston was also the previous owner of the lot. At that time, the area was claimed by the Province of Maryland, and landowners were required to pay taxes (or tithes) to the established Church of England. The new "chapel of ease" at Broad Creek offered local parishioners a more convenient house of worship than the relatively distant mother church of Stepney Parish, located in what is now Wicomico County. The church's subsequent history is summarized in many sources, but there's a bit of a mystery concerning the history of the location prior to 1771.

In Scharf's *History of Delaware*, published in 1888, contributing writer Rev. Benjamin Douglass mentioned an intriguing possibility: "We are inclined to believe that [Christ Church] was not the first building erected on this spot. Tradition points to a prior structure, of which none now can give us any exact information." Some researchers have dismissed the suggestion as just another of the many errors in Scharf's works, but I'm not so sure. There is no known evidence of an earlier Anglican chapel at Broad Creek, but another denomination was active in the area 25+ years before Broad Creek Chapel was built: the Presbyterians.

Is it possible that Old Christ Church stands on or near the site of a forgotten Presbyterian church?

Rev. Charles Tennent, a Presbyterian minister, was preaching at "Broad Creek Bridge" as early as 1747, and a Presbyterian church was built on the northern branch of Broad Creek around 1760. This is the same branch that flows through Chipman's Pond, which was known as Church Creek as early as (and presumably before) the 1790s. I don't know the exact location of this early Presbyterian church; it burned down during the Revolution, and a new church was built at a new location between 1787 and 1791. It's interesting that Robert Houston was a prominent Presbyterian as well as the owner of land adjacent to Church Creek. Perhaps the first Presbyterian church was located on his land. I'd like to learn more.

Three possibilities to consider:

1. It was not unusual for congregations to move churches from one location to another, so it's possible that the poorly documented Presbyterian church built around 1760 stood on the site of Broad Creek Chapel at one time, but was moved prior to 1771.

2. Perhaps the Presbyterian church built around 1760 wasn't the first. Although it's assumed that Tennent was preaching in private homes or outdoors in 1747, it's possible that there was an early Presbyterian church which has been forgotten.

3. More likely, in my opinion, the first Presbyterian church was built *near* the site of Broad Creek Chapel around 1760. Logically, it wouldn't have been located very far from Broad Creek Bridge, so in the mid-1770s, the older Presbyterian church and the new Anglican chapel probably stood near each other. More than a century after the Presbyterian church burned, the locals vaguely remembered their parents and grandparents saying that Old Christ Church was not the first house of worship located next to Church Creek, or Chipman's Pond. This may have been the tradition that Rev. Douglass referred to.

Blackfoot Town (Dagsboro) in Colonial Primary Sources

February 2016

THE EARLY HISTORY of the town of Dagsboro, located in lower Sussex County just off Route 113, is a matter of controversy and speculation, as anyone who has ever googled the subject is aware. Scharf's *History of Delaware* states that the town was known as Blackfoot Town before it was renamed Dagsbury in memory of General John Dagworthy, and subsequent sources have repeated the information. However, specifics concerning the origins of the town and its unusual name are frustratingly elusive, inspiring theories about settlers slogging through black mud, or even Blackfoot Indians.

The purpose of this article is not to comment on those theories, but simply to offer some early primary source references to Blackfoot Town. They're not necessarily the earliest; just the earliest I've stumbled upon. Since the name doesn't appear on any map, the best place to start is colonial land records for Worcester County.

The description of Thomas Dazey's 62-acre tract named Jacob's Neglect, surveyed in 1748, states that the boundaries began "at a marked White Oak standing on the North side of the County Road that leads to blackfoot Town…" This tract was patented to Dazey (or Dasey, presumably one of the forerunners of the local Daisey clan) in 1755. According to Scharf, Thomas Dasey lived in Baltimore Hundred. I'm unsure about the location of the county road; possibilities include roads from Blackfoot Town to Cedar Neck, the Sound, or St. Martin's River and points south.

When the surveyor John Watson traveled to Fenwick's Island in December 1750 to begin surveying and marking the Transpeninsular Line, he mentioned in his journal that the party stopped at Blackfoot Town and "lodged some at one Carters an Inkeeper & one Reads a private House." He described the territory between "Lewis" and Blackfoot as "Barren Grounds," and estimated that the towns were about twenty-two miles apart; a very accurate estimate which proves that the town was, in fact, located on or very near the site of Dagsboro.

Work on the line was suspended nearly a month later due to inclement weather. The party made their way from Romley Marsh across the Head of Sound, then crossed Black Foot Creek on a makeshift bridge of two logs while the horses swam across. They reached Blackfoot Town in the early afternoon, and stayed at Joseph Carter's inn again. Black Foot Creek was probably an early or alternate name for Pepper's Creek or, less likely, Herring Branch, although both names were already in use at that time. Throughout his brief entries, Watson used the spellings: Blackfoot Town, Black foot Town, Blackfoot, and Black foot.

When a 265-acre tract named Red Oak Ridge (not to be confused with unrelated tracts sharing the same name) was resurveyed for Uriah Brookfield in 1756, the first boundary marker was described as "standing on a ridge on the southeast side of the Cyprus Swamp Road about five miles above Blackfoot Town back in the woods & about a mile to the eastward of a cyprus swamp called the Green Swamp…"

Another reference appears in the description of a 100-acre tract named Waples Luck, surveyed for Paul Waples in 1757. Although the wording is a bit confusing, "a County Road leading from Snow Hill to Lewis Town" and "a place called blackfoot Town" are mentioned. This tract may have been adjacent to the town, which might explain the number of Waples households in and around Dagsborough in 1868, according to the Pomeroy & Beers Atlas. Other tracts patented to Paul Waples mention Pepper's Creek. Paul was the son of Peter Waples, who settled on the north Shore of Indian River (Pennsylvania territory) in the 1690s and ran a ferry across the river. The name Ferry Cove still appears on some modern maps.

Yet another reference can be found in a survey for Joshua Burton, dated 1760. His tract named Trouble Reviewed was described as "lying and being in [Worcester County] above black foot Town…" and "near the lower end of the Indian Land…" This is almost certainly a reference to the old reservation known as Askekecky (among other spellings) bordered by today's Indian Town Road, south of Millsboro and northwest of Dagsboro.

Based on these four sources alone, we can be certain that:

1. Blackfoot Town, whatever its origins, was established by 1748.

2. A creek to the south of the town was also named Blackfoot or Black Foot, though it's hard to say which was named first.

3. Joseph Carter ran an inn there in the early 1750s, and a man named Read lived nearby.

4. Paul Waples owned a considerable amount of land near, and possibly in, the town by the late 1750s.

We can probably assume that there were also a couple of mills nearby, and although there's no record of a house of worship prior to the construction of Prince George's Chapel between 1755 and 1757, there were Presbyterian and Anglican churches within a somewhat reasonable distance.

The colonial history of this part of Sussex County is murkier than others. Blackfoot Town, and settlements near the Sound and Fenwick's Island—not to mention the branch of the Sound known as Indian Town Creek—are surely deserving of further research.

Parramore's Plantation at Whaley's Crossroads

January 2019

IT WAS A WARM, sunny afternoon in June of 1769. Defiant Virginians, 37-year-old George Washington among them, had recently taken the bold step of insisting that Great Britain had no right to lay taxes in their colony; on the western frontier, a seasoned hunter named Daniel Boone made his way into the rich, forbidden lands the Shawnee Indians called Cantuck-ee; in the distant Pacific, Captain James Cook sailed amongst the scattered isles of the South Seas; and near the Tub Mill Branch in Broad Creek Forest on the Eastern Shore, Matthew Parramore winced and slapped a mosquito on his exposed neck as he stood and surveyed his new plantation.

He knew the land well, having grown up nearby; he had hunted here as a young man, when it was untouched forest, before James Bouger acquired fifty acres along the old road to Indian River. Like many who tried to build a life in Wimbesoccom Neck, Bouger neither succeeded nor stayed, and most of his land was included in a larger resurvey for John Saunders in 1760. But Saunders inherited his father's land on the east side of the branch, and in less than a decade, sold his own patent land in two parcels. Now Parramore owned one hundred acres of the tract known as Friendship, in addition to his holdings about a mile to the west, near Joseph Collins' mills on Wimbesoccom Creek.

Friendship was not the best land on the peninsula, but it was far from the worst. The ground that had already been cleared was level, and stayed dry most of the time. The wooded northern section was swampy, except during dry spells, but Parramore knew from experience that a strategically located ditch could drain such land well enough for it to be farmed. The first crop he would harvest would be oak, pine, cedar, and bald cypress, as he continued to clear the land and enlarge the existing fields.

He paid little attention to the dwelling house, a small, simple structure with one brick chimney, a roof of cypress shingles, and clapboard siding; and less attention to the cluster of outbuildings behind it. Lumber was plentiful, and new buildings went up quickly with enough help.

The aging planter slapped another mosquito, wiped away the beads of sweat forming on his brow, and turned back towards his horse. There was work to be done.

꙳

THIS SCENE is fueled by imagination, but based on facts. The Parramore family, which had roots in Virginia, settled in Wimbesoccom Neck, north of today's Trap Pond, in the early 1700s. In 1743, just one year after a Nanticoke-led plot to massacre the local English settlers was thwarted, fifty acres near today's Whaley's Crossroads was surveyed for James

Parramore's Plantation

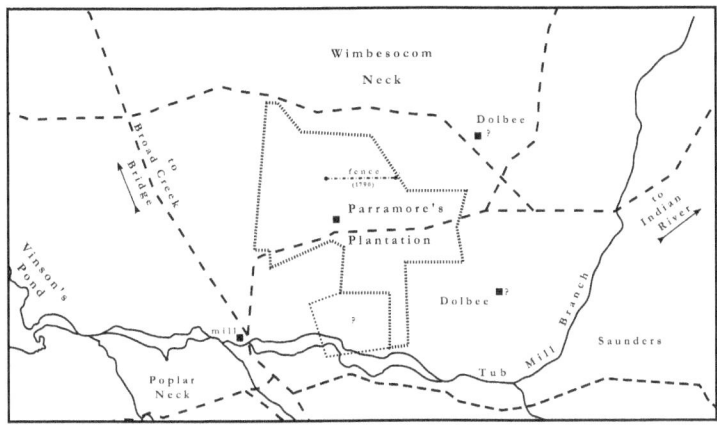

Parramore's Plantation, located near Whaley's Crossroads between today's Laurel and Lowe's Crossroads, circa 1776 – 1790s.

Bouger, who was probably the son of another James Bouger who lived near Broad Creek as early as 1720. Evidently the younger Bouger "omitted paying Caution for the Land," and in 1760 most of the tract was included in a 140-acre resurvey for John N. Saunders. The boundaries of the new tract, called "Friendship," were described as "beginning at a marked red oak tree standing on a level piece of ground back in the woods from Bowgers Mill…"

If the mill is the same one mentioned in a 1740 survey of a tract named "Mill Lot" for Peter Callaway, it was located at Terrapin Pond, and was one of the oldest mills along Broad Creek. It is also possible that there was another mill site elsewhere on the branch.

The adjoining portion of today's Samuel Hill Road seems to have been one of the oldest roads in the neighborhood. As early as 1730, the first bounder of a nearby tract named "Wright's Choice," located alongside the branch, was said to be located "about half a mile below the olde road…" This road was probably one of the primary roads leading northeastward to the head of Indian River (today's Millsboro) during the 18th century.

In 1769, Saunders sold "Friendship" in two parcels: Forty acres to his brother, Andrew Saunders, and one hundred acres to Matthew Parramore. Parramore was not a young man at the time; he was probably in his fifties, if not older. His father, also named Matthew, had died in 1739, aged about 61. He may have expanded his land holdings for the sake of his family's future rather than his own. In 1776, he had the land resurveyed, resulting in the addition of even more adjoining vacant land.

Parramore's will, written in 1783, and the inventory of his estate, compiled in 1784, offer a glimpse into his life during his relatively short time on his new plantation. The will makes it clear that he used it as his dwelling plantation—his home—though he still owned his older lands to the west, where his sons Thomas and Patrick lived. The dwelling plantation would go to a younger son, Ezekiel, when he came of age; in the meantime, Thomas would manage it. The inventory paints a picture of a typical farmer, not wealthy, but secure: No slaves; a few pigs, sheep, and cattle; typical household items like a couple of beds, a spinning wheel, and cookware; and practical tools including a drawing knife, a "shewmakers Hammer," old plows and harrows, and three guns.

The location of Matthew Parramore's grave is unknown. If there was a family burying-ground on the property, which is likely, it has been lost.

For reasons that are unclear, Ezekiel sold the plantation to Thomas on May 23, 1791, for one hundred pounds, with neighbors Peter Dolbee and Jesse Saunders serving as witnesses. Just three weeks later, Thomas sold twenty-two acres to Dolbee; and in November of that year, he conveyed one hundred acres to Jonathan Betts, Sr. It seems likely that neither of these two parcels included the heart of the plantation; i.e., the dwelling house, outbuildings, gardens, etc. However, a little over a year later, in December 1792, he sold an additional seventy-nine acres to Betts, which probably included the oldest and most important part of the plantation, straddling part of today's Samuel Hill Road on the south side of Route 24. The northern boundary of this parcel followed an east-west fence line. In 1793, another fourteen acres, down towards Terrapin Pond, went to Jesse Saunders.

During the 19th century, the old plantation was owned primarily by members of the Betts and Matthews families; notably Henry Clay Matthews, who died in 1917. Subsequently the land was divided into increasingly smaller parcels which changed hands many times. Today members of the Mitchell, Whaley, Hitchens, Slavens, Ellis, Perez, and Hudson families own pieces of the land that Matthew Parramore once called home.

Thornton's map of 1706, oriented with east at the top, shows Whorekill as an alternate name for Cape Henlopen.

Reclaiming Delaware's Unsavory Place-Names: The Whorekill

February 2016

WITHOUT A DOUBT, two of the strangest—and most controversial—place-names in Delaware are Whorekill and Murderkill. Whorekill was an early name for Lewes Creek and the town of Lewes, while the Murderkill River flows through southern Kent County and into the Delaware Bay, and is the source of the names North Murderkill Hundred and South Murderkill Hundred. *Kill* dates back to the Dutch occupation of the region, and simply means "creek." So, Whore Creek? Murder Creek? What's going on here?

As recently as 2014, the *News Journal* published a mythbusting sort of article, assuring readers that the odd names are simply English corruptions of the Dutch terms for Hoorn Creek and Mother Creek, respectively, Hoorn being a Dutch city to which some of the early settlers were connected. Although this seems like a very reasonable explanation—after all, the Dutch *moeder* is fairly similar to the English *murder*, and the name Hornkill does appear in some records—I've come to believe that there is stronger evidence for the names meaning exactly what they seem to mean.

Let's take a look at the Lewes area first, and save Murderkill for another article. The Dutch established the short-lived Zwaanendael settlement there in 1631, and called the creek Blommaert's Kill in honor of Samuel Blommaert, one of the directors of the Dutch West India Company who had purchased the tract from the local Indians, who massacred the settlers shortly thereafter. However, the creek was called Hoeren-kil as early as 1640, and Hoere-kil as early as 1642. *Hoere* means whore, harlot, prostitute, etc., and *hoeren* is simply the plural form of the term; the obvious translation is Whores Creek or Whore Creek.

There was also a Hoeren Eylant (island) in what is now the Connecticut River. Later writers explained both names as

Section of a copy of Jan Jansson's map of the New Netherlands, 1651, erroneously placing Cape Hinlopen at Fenwick Island.

originating from local Indian prostitution or sharing of women.

An alternative, but somewhat speculative translation could be Mud Creek, based on the rather obscure Middle Dutch word *hore* or *hor*, meaning mud, excrement, filth, etc., from the Old High German word *hore*. Interestingly, it has been suggested that both the English *whore* and the Dutch *hoere* could be derived from slang referring to prostitutes as filth or scum. I have never heard or read of anyone suggesting this translation of Whorekill, nor am I arguing in favor of this possibility. I just think it needs to be mentioned, and perhaps investigated further by an authority on 17th-century Dutch.

There is one reason, in particular, that leads me to believe that "whore" is indeed the correct translation, and it requires an understanding of the history of the area. Following the disastrous destruction of Zwaanendael, both the Dutch and the Swedes more or less left the Hoere Kill alone until a Dutch Mennonite named Pieter Plockhoy established a small settlement nearby with forty-one settlers in 1663. The settlement was destroyed by English forces less than a year later, but there is evidence that some of the colonists not only survived the attack, but continued to live in the area. A 1671 census indicates that there were several Dutch households in the town known as Horekill or Whorekill. I'm guessing that the old Hoere Kill became Whorekill not because the English mistranslated a Dutch name, but because the Dutch locals stayed put, became English subjects and learned the language, and translated the name themselves. *Hoere* and *whore* were so similar that the spoken name really didn't even change, only its spelling.

On the other hand, the theory that the creek was named after Hoorn not only requires us to assume that the English botched the name (which would be understandable), but that the Dutch themselves consistently misspelled the name from the very beginning of its use. They did not make this error with other sites named after Hoorn, such as Kaap Hoorn (Cape Horn) in South America. I have trouble believing that Dutch mapmakers who were well aware of the spelling of the important city of Hoorn (see any map of the Netherlands of that period) would have gotten it so badly wrong on maps of the American colony, not only misspelling it but substituting the word for prostitute. I also have trouble believing that rough Dutch seamen, soldiers, fur traders, and the like would have objected to naming a site on the wild frontier after prostitution on moral grounds—particularly since generations of respectable English colonists (and then American citizens) continued to use the name Whorekill even after the town had been renamed Lewes.

It is my position at this time, while keeping an open mind, that the occasional usage of Hornkill in Swedish and English records was an alternative spelling of the original Hoeren-kil, and that the English name Whorekill did, in fact, accurately reflect some association with prostitution. If I were to propose an alternative explanation for the name, I would point to the similar Middle Dutch words for mud, which would make sense in the context of naming a creek. I think the explanation involving the city of Hoorn is the weakest of all, and is perhaps based more on a desire to whitewash history than on primary sources like Dutch maps and records which clearly use Hoeren or Hoere, not Hoorn.

Reclaiming Delaware's Unsavory Place-Names: Murderkill

March 2016

IN A PREVIOUS ARTICLE, I examined the English name Whorekill, which has been explained away as being a corruption of Hoorn (a Dutch city) plus Kill (Dutch for creek), and concluded that the original Dutch name Hoeren-kil or Hoere kill most likely referred to whoring or prostitution on the part of the local Indian women, not the city of Hoorn. I also pointed out that the term *hore* could also be translated "mud" in Middle Dutch, the ancestor of the Dutch language spoken during the era in question.

A similar controversy surrounds the English name Murderkill, which is still in use today. The name dates back to the mid-17th century, when the Dutch and the Swedes had settlements along the Delaware River (then known as the Zuydt Rivier, or South River). *Kill* or *kil* meant creek, but the origin of the name Murder Creek is a bit more complicated.

Confusingly, the river and associated sites (e.g., a Quaker meeting house) were called both Murtherkill and Motherkill (sometimes substituting the suffix -kiln), murther being an archaic term for murder. This lends some credence to the theory that the Dutch originally named the creek Moeder Kill or Mother Creek, which has been advanced in the *News Journal* and elsewhere. The similarity between *moeder* and *murder* is undeniable, but I think the admittedly limited evidence suggests that the creek was named after *murder* (for whatever reason); therefore the English names Murtherkill and Murderkill are accurate successors, and it is Motherkill that was the corruption.

The earliest written form of the name comes from the Swedes. Peter Lindstrom's map of New Sweden, generally agreed to date to the 1650s, includes a waterway labeled Mordare Kijhlen—or, in English, Murderer Creek. The name Moeder Kill or anything similar simply does not appear in any records of the time.

Following the English occupation of the territory in the 1660s, the name became Murther-kill, the English "murther" being an accurate translation of the Swedish *mordar*. This is the earliest English name for the waterway; Motherkill came later.

I believe it was the name and pronunciation of Murtherkill which gave birth to the alternative name Motherkill or Motherkiln. A number of traveling Quakers wrote of visiting the Motherkill or Motherkiln meeting during the mid- to late 1700s. Yet the names Murtherkill and Murderkill also appear in records of that era. Although I haven't examined all of the sources in which the various names appear, based on those I've read it seems like locals and official records tended to use Murtherkill or Murderkill more often, which visiting preachers and the like may have misheard as Motherkill. For example, William Reckitt mentioned attending a meeting at

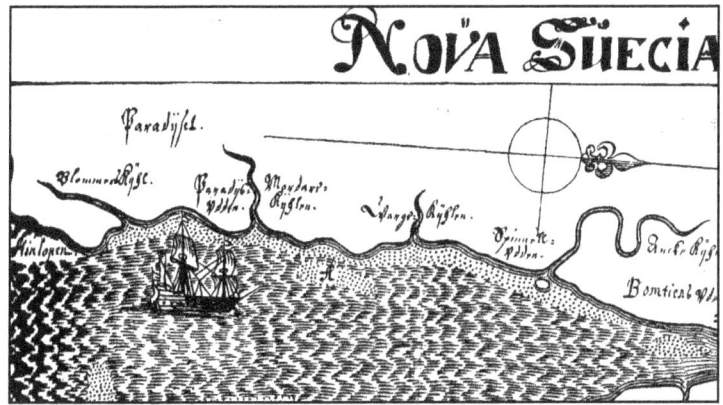

Published in 1691, Lindestrom's map is believed to date to the 1650s. Notice Hinlopen at the far left or southernmost portion of the map.

Motherkill in 1758. In 1763, Daniel Stanton recorded the name as Mother-kiln, and in 1766, John Woolman spelled the name Motherkill. Job Scott recorded the name Mother-kill as late as 1790, yet the local abolitionist Warner Mifflin mentioned the Murtherkill Meeting in 1797. Generally speaking, the creek or river tended to be called Murderkill more often than the other variations during this period, and it is this name that survives to this day.

As to why the Dutch and/or Swedes named a creek after murder or murderers, vague legends involving a massacre of the local Indians have surfaced in sources of questionable reliability, but even the earliest references to these legends seem highly speculative, and were perhaps more an attempt to explain an odd name than to preserve genuine traditions.

DELAWARE DAY:
NOT THE FIRST STATE

December 2015

> *"Since 1933, the governors of Delaware have proclaimed December 7 as Delaware Day in honor of that day in 1787, when Delaware became the first state to ratify the Federal Constitution, thus making Delaware the first state in the New Nation."*
>
> – State of Delaware official website, 2015

SO GOES TINY DELAWARE's favorite claim to fame, aside from the duPont family, and, in some circles, Joe Biden: Delaware was the first to ratify the U.S. Constitution, thereby becoming the first state.

But it's not true.

Although it *is* true that Delaware was the first state to ratify the Consitution, it had already been a state for eleven years at that point, and it wasn't the oldest. Rhode Island's colonial legislature declared independence from Great Britain on May 4, 1776; the legislature of the Three Lower Counties of Pennsylvania, home to more than their fair share of Loyalists, did not follow suit until June 15th. This date marks the separation of New Castle, Kent, and Sussex Counties from Pennsylvania as well as Great Britain, and is still remembered and celebrated as Separation Day.

The new state adopted a constitution on September 20, 1776, which officially established the name "the Delaware State." In the following years, life went on. War raged through the colonies. In February 1779, the Delaware State become the next to last to ratify the Articles of Confederation. The war formally ended in 1783, shortly after Delaware had begun its eighth year of statehood. George Washington was revered as a war hero. In Sussex County, the farmers who had opposed independence tilled their fields, their daily lives largely unchanged.

Finally, in December 1787, ten delegates from each county met in Dover to consider a proposed federal constitution, which would establish a new national government. The delegates from Sussex County were John Ingram of Broadkill Hundred; John Jones and Israel Holland of Baltimore Hundred; Thomas Laws of Northwest Fork Hundred; Woodman Stockley of Indian River Hundred; John Laws, Jr., of Nanticoke Hundred; Thomas Evans of Cedar Creek Hundred; and William Moore, William Hall, and Isaac Cooper of Little Creek Hundred.

On December 7, the thirty delegates unanimously voted to ratify the Constitution, stating:

> *"We the Deputies of the People of the Delaware State, in Convention met, having taken into our serious consideration the Federal Constitution proposed and agreed upon by the Deputies of the United States in a General Convention held at the City of Philadelphia on the*

seventeenth day of September in the year of our Lord one thousand seven hundred and eighty seven, Have approved, assented to, ratified, and confirmed, and by these Presents, Do, in virtue of the Power and Authority to us given for that purpose, for and in behalf of ourselves and our Constituents, fully, freely, and entirely approve of, assent to, ratify, and confirm the said Constitution."

It is this resolution, and its influence upon other states which were debating the proposed Constitution, which should be celebrated on Delaware Day—not Delaware's statehood, which was already old, old news on December 7, 1787; and not the achievement of becoming the first American state, which Delaware didn't achieve anyway.

Richard Fish Cadle
1796 – 1857

Reverend Richard F. Cadle: A Brief Profile

August 2015

RICHARD FISH CADLE was born in New York in 1796. As a teenager he studied at Columbia College, and went on to become an important Episcopal minister and missionary, known especially for founding churches in the wild territories of Michigan and Wisconsin. He came to Laurel, Delaware, in the spring of 1853 following the resignation of the Reverend James W. Hoskins, and assumed responsibility for the Protestant Episcopal parishes at Seaford, Broad Creek, and Little Hill.

The churches under Rev. Cadle's care included Christ Church, located a couple of miles northeast of the village of Laurel, and considered the mother church of the Episcopal churches of western Sussex County; St. Luke's, located in Seaford; the recently completed St. Philip's, a chapel in Laurel which quickly became more popular with parishioners than the comparably distant mother church; and St. John's at Little

Hill, a tiny chapel located about seven miles east of Laurel.

Rev. Cadle was given a house and $150 in cash, and was supplied with hogs and corn by some of the local farmers. Although the previous rector had been given two slaves, it is assumed that the vestry probably sold or freed them due to Cadle's opposition to slavery. One of his first services in Laurel was the burial service of Joseph O'Neal, who had died in late March at age seventy.

Although he was not considered an exceptional preacher, due to a minor speech impediment, Rev. Cadle was known as an educated man, a gifted writer, and a passionate teacher, establishing a class in Laurel for the study of "approved religious books," a Bible study class, and Sunday Schools for children. Of course, he also performed all of the regular duties of an Episcopal minister, presiding over marriages, baptisms, funerals, and burials, not only at the churches he served, but also at Methodist and Presbyterian churches, and in private residences. At that time, Methodism was by far the dominant faith in the area. In early 1857, he organized St. Mark's in Little Creek Hundred, a few miles south of Laurel, which initially met at a private residence.

During the time of Rev. Cadle's ministry, Christ Church, which was already nearly ninety years old, was in rather poor condition, and he hoped that the historic house of worship would be repaired and maintained, writing, "It is earnestly to be wished that the object of so much nursing care may yet be a joy of many generations."

After being caught out in a cold storm in October 1857, apparently while performing his duties, Rev. Cadle became ill, and died in a parishioner's home on November 9th. Reportedly, his final words were, "The blood of Christ is sufficient for all things."

The Journal of
Rev. John Milton Purner

Spring 2019

On the morning of January 29, 1860, a Sunday, the folks who lived around Lowe's Crossroads filled their pews at Jones M. E. Church. Rev. John Milton Purner, who had stayed with Isaac Short the night before, preached on Hebrews 6:1. He appreciated the large crowd and good atmosphere. After the service, the 26-year-old minister rode his horse northwestward towards Terrapin Hill, probably dining with a parishioner along the way. Another service was held at Bethesda M. E. Church, where he preached on II Corinthians 8:9 to the largest congregation that had gathered there all year. After a less successful evening service at Bethesda featuring a sermon on Romans 2:4-5, Purner spent the night at the nearby home of Hezekiah Matthews.

The details of this typical Sunday are preserved in the *Journal of the Rev. John Milton Purner: January – May 1860*, a new addition to the Laurel Historical Society's collection.

The journal was transcribed and edited by Barbara Duffin and Philip Lawton for the Commission on Archives and History of the Peninsula-Delaware Conference of The United Methodist Church, and published in 2004. Copies can be purchased at Barratt's Chapel & Museum of Methodism in Frederica, which holds the original.

Born in Cecil County, Maryland, Purner entered the ministry in his twenties and spent a year in training on the Lewes Circuit before coming to Laurel in 1859. As a Junior Preacher, he did not have a house of his own, but depended on church members for meals and lodging. He preached at St. Thomas, Jones, Bethesda, Hepburn (King's), Old Zion (colored), Mount Zion, Bethel, and St. George's, among other local churches. His brief entries—which are rife with misspellings, but usually readable—include sermon texts, comments about services, and the names of his hosts. Typically, he only stayed with a family for a night or two before moving on. On more than one occasion, the young man wrote that he was homesick.

Reading between the lines, one wonders at the amount of attention Purner seems to have received from young women, and how it might have affected him, a young man in his late twenties. Consider the entry from January 18th:

> *Leave for Br E. Hitches take dinner Miss Collins their visiting spend it after noon in righting – spend in eving 'th the girles vey plesently – a day of dark temptation from the Devil.. Spend the even studing Watson –*

A number of other entries mention visits from single women, often in groups of two or three—or more, as was the case on February 14th:

> *Studing Watson –&c interrupted with visiters Miss E.*

Cannon, Miss E. Gordy Miss Mary Mathews, Mar Cannon Magge Collens, Kati Collens poor chance to study without a home ~ go to class good tim Reeceve a letter from Sister Marria heare of Rebecca illness ~ ~ all Night at Cap Lewes the girlle stay all Night to dark to go home.

Though Purner's brief notes probably contain little of interest to those who aren't familiar with the churches he preached at or the families he stayed with, they nonetheless offer a rare glimpse into the daily life of a young Methodist circuit rider in the Laurel area and the people who inhabited that life.

By April 1860, Purner had been assigned to the Church Creek Circuit, and subsequently served in other communities on the peninsula, including Sharptown and Accomac. Sadly, he died on a Sunday morning in 1867 at age 34. The journal he kept during his time in Laurel, despite its brevity, is a valuable contribution to the history of the community.

QUIET SUNDAY AT "OLD FORGE"

LAUREL, Del., Aug. 3—"Old Forge," the leading negro camp of the peninsula, two miles from Laurel, broke up yesterday morning after a ten days' encampment.

This has been the camp's most successful year, and the first year to be free from shootings and of free fights. Five white Methodist camps within a radius of fifteen miles of Laurel opened yesterday.

The *Evening Journal,* August 3, 1909

Old Forge A.M.E. Church & Camp

January 2020

OLD FORGE A. M. E. CHURCH *was located beside James' Branch a short distance s. w. of the old Broad Creek Bridge. Near this point, a forge, a saw-mill and a grist-mill were erected in the late 1700s. The forge was the first to be abandoned, the saw-mill was closed about 1880 and the grist-mill was closed some time later.*

On Sept. 16, 1848, James Horsey donated a half-acre church site to a group of free Africans headed by Samson Mathews. Old Forge Church was built and a graveyard was laid out. An active camp-meeting was conducted each year in the woods beside the church. The church was closed about 1909 and the land reverted to Wm. De Shields who had purchased the Horsey farm. There were no tombstones in the graveyard and there is nothing to mark the old site.

– Frank R. Zebley, *The Churches of Delaware*, 1947

It is unclear when, exactly, Frank R. Zebley wrote this entry in his wonderful book, since he spent years researching, visiting, and photographing hundreds of Delaware churches before its publication, but some of his photos of Laurel-area churches date to the mid-1930s, a mere twenty years after the annual camp meeting at Old Forge was said to be one of the most popular black camp meetings on the entire peninsula. It seems unthinkable that all visible evidence of a church, campground, and cemetery—the center of a community for countless people over several generations—could vanish so quickly, and that so little of its history would be remembered.

Yet even today, with easy access to newspapers and other records via searchable online databases, we have only been able to learn a little more of that history. Most of the story of Old Forge A.M.E. remains unknown.

It begins, as Zebley stated, in 1848. For the sum of ten dollars (the site wasn't truly donated), James and Bridget Horsey sold one-half acre of land to trustees "Samson Matthews, Isaac Rodney, Isaac Morris, George Polk, William Sipple, John Saunders, Peter Truitt and Robert Sipple free Africans" under the condition that they would build "a house or place of worship for the use of the African people. . ."

The rectangular lot was described as beginning at "a post on east side of a road leading from Polk Mills (originally) down the western side of said Mill Branch out into the state road leading from Georgetown to Salisbury Maryland and intersecting said road near Broad Creek Bridge so called and then running from said post along or nearly along the East side of said road. . ." Like the church, these roads no longer exist, and the entire site is shrouded in forest.

Little is known of most of the trustees. There were two "free colored" men named Samson Matthews living in Sussex County at the time. John Saunders was involved in the Union

Temperance Benevolent Society. The most prominent trustee, by far, seems to be William Sipple, a successful Laurel blacksmith and landowner who provided land to Mt. Pisgah A.M.E., served as a trustee of the local African-American school, and is even believed to have been involved in the Underground Railroad.

Although it is assumed that the new church was named Old Forge A.M.E. upon its construction, the name does not appear on the deed. Evidently the church began holding annual camp meetings in 1855, but we only know this because the camp celebrated its 60th anniversary in 1915; the known records are silent about both church and camp meeting during the early decades. Hopefully, more information will be discovered.

As if to make up for years of inattention, somebody began submitting brief notes about the camp to the newspapers in the early 20th century. On July 23, 1902, Wilmington's *Every Evening* reported that Old Forge camp meeting was in progress and drawing a large attendance. The same article implies that some of the attendees were robbing nearby watermelon fields under the cover of darkness, while farmers guarded their fields with shotguns. Three weeks later, on August 15th, *Every Evening* reported that Old Forge was still drawing a crowd from Laurel. That's some camp meeting!

Alleged watermelon heists paled in comparison to the news that came from the camp two years later. After a violent brawl erupted in or near the campground, during which knives, blackjacks, razors, and pistols were brandished if not actually used, participant Lee Ackwood—a rough character who makes several appearances in Maryland and Delaware newspapers for various crimes—returned to the camp later that evening and shot John White, a popular and respected black merchant, badly injuring him. Both the *Morning News* and the *Philadelphia Inquirer* reported that a posse searched for Ackwood on the night of the crime, but the latter clarified that the posse consisted of black men: "…if caught he will be lynched by his own race, as White was extremely popular, and his friends are determined to wreak vengeance upon his assailant." The shooter was arrested and jailed the next morning.

The camp continued to have a tainted reputation; the ten-day meeting in 1909 was said to be the first without shootings or fights. It seems that the church was closed at about this time—probably due, in part, to the condition of the aging structure—for in 1910 the annual camp meeting was continued by Mt. Pisgah A.M.E. Church. In 1914, the *Morning News* contradicted the various reports of violent incidents, stating that the camp had "always been free from shooting scrapes." The 60th annual camp meeting, in 1915, was described as one of the most successful in the camp's history—yet it also seems to have marked the end of the camp's history. Old Forge is conspicuously absent from state newspapers after 1915. The seemingly abrupt demise of the camp corresponds with a peninsula-wide crackdown on black camp meetings due to a perception that they frequently turned disorderly or violent. Prejudice was certainly a factor, but, surprisingly, some black ministers were in agreement, citing alcohol use, gambling, and arrests at so-called "bush meetings."

Whether the camp was affected by new legal restrictions or it simply couldn't survive without an active church at the site, its closing marked the end of an era in the community. With its lost cemetery and incomplete history, the wooded site of Old Forge A.M.E. Church in today's state-owned James Branch Nature Preserve continues to be one of the most intriguing locations in Laurel.

Terrapin Hill
& Bull's Mills

2014

IF YOU WERE TO TRAVEL from the thriving town of Laurel to Gumborough during the Civil War, you would not take today's Route 24 to Lowe's Crossroads. You couldn't. At that time, the main road ran roughly parallel to what was known as the main branch of Broad Creek, veering southeast shortly after Bull's Mills, about six miles east of town. A mile farther, and you'd be at Terrapin Hill, a low hill that was probably prime real estate during the colonial era, when the surrounding area was part of the Pocomoke or Cypress Swamp and the local landowners were still working to drain it with a network of ditches. There was a community there, smaller than a village, but busier than the typical country crossroads; there were four intersections within a quarter mile, and about thirty houses within a one-mile radius.

Terrapin Hill appears on a map published in 1856. I'm not sure how old the name was at that time. In *Folklore of Sussex*

County, Delaware, Dorothy W. Pepper stated that the name was of Indian origin, but didn't elaborate. I suspect she meant that terrapin is an Algonquian word, not that the Nanticokes named this specific location after terrapins.

There was a sawmill at Terrapin Pond, and another at nearby Raccoon Pond, which were owned by various members of the Hudson, Matthews, Wootten, and Cannon families over the years. The nearest gristmill and post office were back at Bull's Mills. Two stores offered whatever the residents didn't make or grow themselves. Most attended Bethesda M. E. Church, which had been built in 1823, but the slightly older St. John's at Little Hill, a small Episcopal chapel, was only about a mile away. Children learned to read and write at the one-room Bethesda schoolhouse. From Terrapin Hill, you could travel south to Whitesville, southeast to Gumborough, or northeast to Lowe's Crossroads and Millsborough—in the unlikely event that you needed or wanted to.

A century and a half later, little remains of the once-vibrant community at Terrapin Hill. The stores, mills, and schoolhouse are all gone, as are all but one of the old farmhouses. Bethesda M. E. Church, which was replaced in 1879, has been beautifully restored, but St. John's was converted into a private residence a few years ago. Even the roads have changed; part of the old road to Little Hill has been a driveway for decades, and the road to Lowes Crossroads has vanished completely. Terrapin Hill still shows up on some modern maps, but the name is meaningless to most locals, little more than the fading ghost of a forgotten community.

BY THE CIVIL WAR, the sawmill and gristmill named after Manaen Bull, a former British soldier who married Governor Nathaniel Mitchell's widow, were already more than one hundred years old, having been built by Joseph Collins before 1760, when the area was still claimed by Maryland. They were built on a branch of Broad Creek known as Wimbesoccom Creek during the colonial era, Sockum Creek during the late 18th and early 19th centuries, and Gray's Branch from about the 1850s to the present. In modern terms, they were located on the south side of Laurel Road (Route 24) immediately before the road to Trap Pond, though at that time that road didn't exist and the Trap Mills were relatively unimportant.

There were only about a dozen houses clustered around Bull's Mills, but the surrounding area was populated enough to justify a post office and schoolhouse. The nearest church was Bethesda M.E. Church, about a mile and a half to the southeast, but there was also a new Methodist Protestant (M.P.) congregation meeting in another schoolhouse, only about a mile to the northeast. They would eventually build their own church and name it Trinity.

It seems that there was a sizable black population in the area between Bull's Mills and Hitchens' Crossroads, about two miles north. In *The Churches of Delaware*, Frank R. Zebley briefly mentioned that "Gray's Church, colored" was "located south of Record's School near Gray's Branch," but offered no additional information. An A.M.E. church was built across from the Ross Point Colored School in 1884, on what is now East Trap Pond Road. I'm not sure how old the schoolhouse (which was replaced in 1922) was; it doesn't appear on the Pomeroy & Beers Atlas of 1868, but the atlas isn't perfect. Unfortunately, historians have tended to overlook 19th-century black churches, schools, and communities, particularly in rural areas.

Today you will not find the name Bull's Mills on any map. Or Bull's anything, for that matter. The community became known as Pepper's Store or simply Pepper, and the old mill-pond was named Pepper Pond. The mills, store, and schoolhouse are long gone.

A Brief History of Trap Pond

August 2016

Trap Pond has long been a favorite destination in the Laurel area. With a large campground, shady picnic areas, a network of trails, boating, public hunting areas, and—in simpler times when water quality wasn't a concern—swimming areas, our local state park has served as a tranquil oasis of sorts, offering generations of families a respite from an increasingly busy world, and a taste of nature.

Yet Trap Pond wasn't always associated with recreation. It wasn't always named Trap Pond. In fact, it wasn't always a pond. The early history of the site is, like its waters, a bit murky, but scattered clues in old records tell its story.

When English surveyors began laying out tracts of land for aspiring tobacco planters along the branches of Broad Creek in the late 1600s and early 1700s, the area was part of a wild frontier. The land was swampy, black bears roamed the woods, and Nanticoke Indians outnumbered the white newcomers.

In 1730, a 100-acre tract named Forest Chance was surveyed on the southwest side of what is now Trap Pond, but the site was simply described as "the main branch of broad creek." It's unclear who dammed the creek near the northern boundary of Forest Chance or exactly when they did it (possibly a Collins or Stevens in the mid-1700s), but by 1791, Newbold Vinson, Sr., owned a sawmill and a gristmill there. The mills stayed in the Vinson family for the next couple of decades, and during that time the pond that powered them was known as Vinson's Pond. However, by 1816, the mills were owned by Joseph Betts, and the pond was named after him.

In the following years, deeds referred to the millpond by both names. In 1836, for example, William Hitch purchased a share of "a certain saw mill and grist mill called and known by the name of the Vinson or Betts mill" from John Betts. However, just four years later, Hitch and Philip Short sold Ebenezer Gray "one third part of…a certain saw and grist mill house & lot adjoining said mills known by the name of Vinsons Mills (now called the Trap Mills)…" The origin of this new name—which, as we know, stuck—is uncertain, and has inspired creative yet unlikely theories involving a trapiche distillery, a tract of land named Turkey Trap (which was actually located elsewhere), or even French Trappist monks, but one possible explanation is that the pond became known as a trap because it collected unwanted runoff from an extensive network of drainage ditches. Now that the mills were co-owned by multiple investors, naming them after a particular individual or family may have been impractical. Henceforth they were known as the Trap Mills.

In his *History of Delaware*, published in 1888, J. Thomas Scharf (or an uncredited contributor) reported that the sawmill was no longer used, but the gristmill was owned and operated by M. G. Truitt. The gristmill continued to operate until 1920.

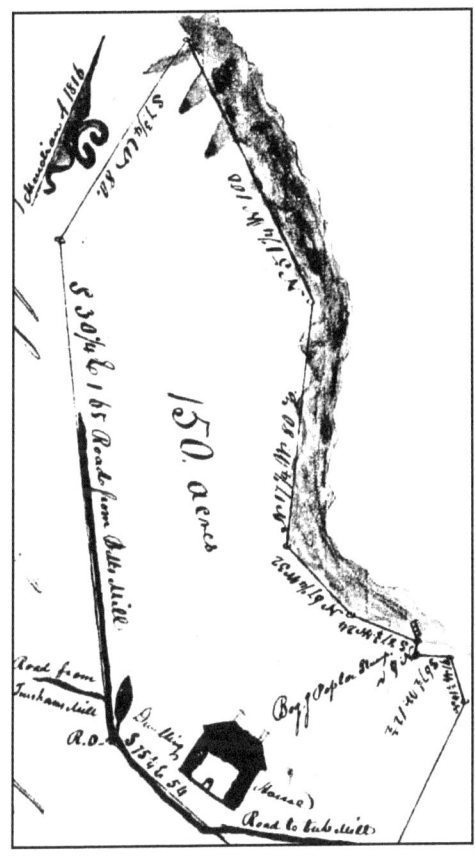

Surveyor's plat of the tract "Forest Chance" in 1816, with nearby roads, a house, and the pond itself.

It should be noted that during this era, Trap Pond was an industrial site, valued for its milling power, location, and resources rather than its beauty. In the early years, the pond had been full of trees, which were eventually harvested along with most of the surrounding timber, leaving behind acres of unsightly, slowly rotting stumps. Such was the scene in 1933, when a devastating flood washed out the old mill dam. Subsequently the federal government bought the pond and surrounding land, and set about creating a recreation area. Between 1936 and 1938 the Civilian Conservation Corps removed the old stumps, rebuild the dam, created small beaches, and built bath houses, park benches, and pavilions, which attracted thousands of visitors in the following years. In 1951, the State of Delaware acquired the pond from the federal government and established the state's first active state park.

Today Trap Pond State Park is larger than ever, consisting of 3,653 acres, including nearby Trussum Pond (another early millpond), the historic Bethesda M. E. Church and cemetery, smaller cemeteries created by the Wingate and Warrington families, and old public roads that survive as trails, all of which have their own stories and are important parts of the history of our community.

Red Hannah: Delaware's Whipping Post

July 2020

I ORDERED A COPY of *Red Hannah: Delaware's Whipping Post* by Robert Graham Caldwell, published in 1947, when I learned that there was a movement afoot to remove the historic whipping post in Georgetown due to its alleged racist symbolism. Unfortunately, two-day shipping wasn't fast enough to beat the mad dash to topple any Delaware monument with an alleged connection to racism, and the book arrived after the post had already been removed. On the day of its removal, nearly every newspaper in the country ran a gushing story about how Delaware was *finally* removing this relic of oppression. Reportedly a crowd gathered and cheered.

    I was surprised by the haste with which the state acted, and vaguely skeptical of the argument that there was something inherently racist about the presence of the whipping post as an educational display. This was more of a gut feeling than an informed opinion on my part. I'd never heard anyone complain about the post before. Surely it had been used to punish whites and blacks alike. . . right? But I didn't have any facts at my disposal, so I bit my tongue and hoped that I'd find answers in the book.

Red Hannah is an unapologetically biased and opinionated book aimed at the abolition of public whipping as a form of punishment in Delaware, which was still legal (but rare) when it was written. The preface offers this radical suggestion: "What is needed is not the replacement of whipping with some other method of punishment, but the elimination of all methods of punishment not only in Delaware but everywhere in the United States, and the introduction of a system of scientific treatment…" So Caldwell makes it very clear from the start that he is opposed to punishing criminals, and considers whipping to be an especially barbaric punishment.

The book is well-researched and includes extensive endnotes. Caldwell begins by tracing the history of whipping in Delaware from the Dutch and Swedish settlements through the English colonial era. During this period, corporal punishment was common, and imprisonment was rare. Criminals convicted of a variety of offenses could expect to be pilloried and/or whipped in a public setting. The humiliation of being ridiculed by an audience was intended to be part of the punishment. In the nineteenth century, imprisonment became common, but Delaware continued to use the whipping post and the pillory, even as other states outlawed them. Caldwell and many of his sources repeatedly condemn whipping as brutal, barbaric, and ineffective. The other side argued that the punishment deterred crime.

This portion of the book, covering the 17th through 19th centuries, does not focus on race. Whipping was a punishment for specific crimes, and whites and blacks who were convicted of these crimes were whipped. In fact, the book

lists two groups of men who were whipped in New Castle County in the late 19th century, and most of them were white. Although Caldwell provides many examples of criticism of the practice, the criticism is based on the supposed cruelty of the punishment. The historical illustrations in the book also depict both white and black criminals going under the lash. It seems to me that, in general and probably with some exceptions, whipping as a punishment was not deliberately aimed at black Delawareans during this period.

Delaware finally abolished the pillory in 1905, but clung to the whipping post despite continuing controversy. It is at this point that Caldwell is able to offer and analyze detailed statistics about the use of the whipping post in the 20th century. From 1900 to 1942, more than 7,000 prisoners were convicted of crimes punishable by whipping (and the racial breakdown was about half and half), but only 22% of them were whipped. Of this minority, 66% were black. From 1940 to 1942, 80% of the prisoners who were whipped (36 out of a total of 45) were black. These are the statistics that have been used in modern times to support the argument that the whipping post was employed in a discriminatory fashion against blacks. This seems like a reasonable conclusion on the surface; racist white judges were more likely to order black convicts to be whipped, right? However, Caldwell offers a different explanation, citing New Castle County statistics which indicate that repeat offenders were more likely to be whipped, and there was a higher percentage of black repeat offenders. So, despite Caldwell's fierce opposition to whipping, he concludes that the court of the 1940s did not directly discriminate against blacks in ordering whippings, while admitting that other social factors, including discrimination, probably caused black criminals to become repeat offenders and therefore be more likely to be whipped.

By 1942, fewer than 7% of criminals convicted of a crime punishable by whipping actually got whipped. So the vast majority of black convicts were never whipped, a fact which challenges the portrayal of the whipping post as a tool of institutional racism.

It is important to note that during this period, all of the crimes punishable by whipping also carried a prison sentence. So, whether a criminal was whipped or not, he still went to prison. In my opinion, this is where Caldwell's argument (as well as that of modern critics of the whipping post) falls apart: A whipping consisting of ten to twenty lashes, or rarely more, and lasting for only a few minutes, is considered to be cruel and unusual, but throwing the same criminal into prison for years of his life is not. I completely disagree. Personally, I think whipping is the lesser of the two punishments by far. Even if Delaware judges were deliberately singling out black convicts for whippings during the first half of the 20th century, which is possible, the brief but painful whipping was a relatively minor add-on to a lengthy and life-shattering prison sentence, which was the true punishment.

Caldwell doubles down on his radical opposition to criminal punishment in the last chapter of the book, urging the adoption of experimental methods of "scientific treatment" of criminals which he does not explain. In the 1940s, this probably seemed like a progressive, enlightened position, full of promise. From my perspective in 2020, when the U.S. has the highest rate of imprisonment in the world, beating even communist China, it seems arrogantly naïve.

Red Hannah: Delaware's Whipping Post is an important slice of Delaware history, but it is primarily a work of opinion; its historical documentation serves to support the author's opinion, and is secondary in importance. The central point of the book, written in 1947, is that Delaware should stop whipping prisoners. The author's dream became reality in a couple of decades; the last whipping was carried out in the 1960s, and the practice was officially abolished in 1972. Therefore, much of the book feels obsolete from today's perspective, but the historical sections are well-researched, and, overall, the book is a useful addition to our knowledge of Delaware history and a welcome addition to my bookshelf.

About the Author

Chris Slavens lives in Laurel, Delaware, with his wife, Crystal. He has contributed to numerous publications including the *News Journal*, the *Laurel Star*, and the *Libertarian Republic*, and is the author of *The Roofed Graves of Delmarva*. He founded Bald Cypress Books in 2020 to publish books about the Delmarva Peninsula, including historical reprints. Currently Chris serves on the board of directors of the Laurel Historical Society, and edits the society's newsletter. He is also a member of the Independent Book Publishers Association.

In addition to writing and publishing, Chris enjoys reading, gardening, hunting, and playing bass guitar.

www.ingramcontent.com/pod-product-compliance
Lightning Source LLC
Chambersburg PA
CBHW040424100526
44589CB00022B/2818